DAY WORK TO DUTY

Bruce E. Robinson

Acknowledgments

I was able to complete this literary project only with the assistance of my team of experts. Many thanks to Robert Catalanotti for lending his superb knowledge of publishing and his professional expertise to the project. Thanks to Paul Oparowski, lee print + design, who labored diligently to design the book cover and craft the proper layout. No publication should go to press without review by a professional editor. I thank my editor, Diane Hinckley, for her sharp eyes and keen professional editing skills. Thanks again, team. And thanks to all who have offered their support to the project.

DAY WORK TO DUTY

By: Bruce E. Robinson

FOREWORD

My name is Bruce E. Robinson. I am the last born of five children, as a result of the union of David Robinson and Margaret Christopher, whose paths crossed in a small community just outside of Philadelphia, Pennsylvania. I am also known as Robbie.

I have made a few observations during my life's journey. If you focus too much on the future, you may miss the pleasures and bounty of the present. We are admonished by God's Word to be content in whatever state we are in. However, contentment must not be confused with complacency. Contentment is about attitude and appreciation. It requires humility, patience, and perseverance. Contentment is operating in the now with a positive attitude while simultaneously preparing for the future. It is having goals and visions and using sound principles to build a solid foundation for the future. It is bypassing shortcuts and following the trail blazed by our predecessors. It includes doing one's present job enthusiastically as if it is the most important thing in the world, while having the assurance that it is a temporary stop along one's life journey. It is not the work we do, but how we do the work that leads to enhanced opportunities.

This book was inspired by the courageous Soldiers of the 98th Division (Iroquois Warriors), whose selfless service motivated and inspired me. I have shared part of my story with them, and they have encouraged me to disclose the rest. So on behalf of my Iroquois Warrior Family, I offer my simple story. God is Good!

Author's note: I solicited information regarding my family history from my mother, Margaret Christopher Robinson and paternal aunt, Florence Robinson Assenheimer. They provided the following.

AS RELATED BY MARGARET

I was sent to stay with my Grandma Annie Johnson, my maternal grandmother, at an early age after a schoolteacher took a dislike to me and singled me out for abusive punishment. My Grandma Sallie Christopher, my paternal grandmother, wasn't going to have that teacher abuse the students, and eventually led the effort to have her removed. One day while at grandma's house she sent me to the old country store to get something – lard, I think. While I was at the store, the owner asked me if I knew how to pluck a chicken. I said, "Yes, Ma'am," and plucked the chicken. In those days if a white person asked you to do something you did it. The lady gave me some candy and a quarter for plucking the chicken. I thought I was rich. I had taken so long that grandma sent my Uncle William for me. He never showed up, so he must have done something else. I took the quarter home and hide it the floor of a closet and enjoyed the candy. William must have found that quarter and spent it, because I never say it again.

I was sent to Philadelphia on Labor Day weekend in 1939. I was seventeen. My Aunt Alease and her husband had come to Virginia with their new baby and were heading back to Philadelphia when my grandmother opened the car door and said, "Margaret, get in. I'm sending you to Philadelphia. There is no future around here in Brunswick County. Sometimes you get paid, sometimes you don't. I want you to have a better life." I protested because I didn't have any shoes. She sent me anyway. My aunt Marie also wanted me in Philadelphia to help with her brother. My Uncle Albertis had undergone kidney surgery. Marie taught me how to use the telephone and gas stove. I was to look after Albertis after his kidney surgery. Shortly after he was brought home his stitches started to break and I had to call for the ambulance to take him back to the hospital. I applied direct pressure to the wound, which the doctor said probably saved his life. That was the first of my nursing duties. I didn't suspect I would later have to take care of Dave (Dad) for twenty-three plus years, and then my mother.

Young people don't believe me when I tell them I made $2.50 a week when I first started to work. I stayed with a white family and was supposed to work five days a week, but it was usually seven days. Then on the days I was off I had to pay carfare to go anyplace, so I didn't really make any money.

It was my Aunt Catherine who was responsible for my meeting Dad. She had come to Jenkintown, just outside of Philadelphia, from Virginia in 1940 to attend high school there, because there was no public high school in Virginia for blacks back then. There was this little club in Elkins Park where we used to go to buy a sandwich or soda. It had these long steps. Sometimes the boys would come over from Ambler to play Jenkintown in football and everyone would say, "There's Rob, that good football player from Ambler." I was over by the bus the boys rode from Ambler, and Rob used to ask me my name. I would tell him I don't have a name, and ignore him. Then he would come to the little club and ask, "Where is the lady with the pretty hair?" Whenever I would see him coming into the little club I would leave. One time I saw him coming and ducked under the tables to avoid him as I tried to get to the back door. I went tearing down those long steps, and he started after me. I then fell into a hole and couldn't get out. I had started to gain a little weight back then, and the more I tried to get out the hole, the deeper I sank. He asked if he could help and I kept telling him no until I was so far gone that he and his buddy had to pull me out of the hole.

I had scratches and bruises all over me. The ladies on the bus asked, "What happened to you? Did your husband beat you up?" I said, "No, I don't have a husband. I fell in a hole." Anyway, I couldn't get rid of Rob. When we were first married we lived in a one room flat in Philly and he worked driving a meat truck before being drafted into the Army. Eleanor came along, and then the war, and Dave. After the war, and with five kids, Dad started working at the asbestos plant in Ambler.

I had a feeling something was going to happen the day Dad got hurt because we had an argument. We were living in the projects on the second floor on Brown Place. I had a vision of him falling down some steps. At the plant where he worked he operated a crane. There were two ceiling cranes that operated on parallel rails next to each other. What happened was the guy who operated the other crane was mad at Dad and started moving his crane toward him as he was getting into his crane's cab. It tore Dad's abdomen open, along with his hip, leg, and knee. His arm was broken, and I think some of his intestines were pulled out. They took him to Germantown Hospital, where the doctors didn't expect him to live. He was given up for dead several times. I will never forget his doctor, Dr. Henry Knox, who never gave up trying to save him. He was the best surgeon in Philadelphia. Miraculously, Dad pulled through the surgeries. But another doctor told me that he would be an invalid and that I would have to push him in a wheelchair for the rest of his life. I told the doctor that he was wrong and that Dad was not going to be an invalid. That doctor didn't like Dad, and accused him of not trying hard enough to recover. Dad desperately wanted to leave that hospital after he began to get better. Dr. Knox ordered Dad to stay in the hospital. But when Dr. Knox left on vacation the doctor who didn't like dad released him. I brought him home in a cabilance. When Dr. Knox returned from vacation he came to our house, furious. "David Robinson," he said, "didn't I tell you that you were not to leave the hospital?" Then when Dr. Knox saw five little heads peeking around the corner, he said, "Oh, I see why you had to leave the hospital."

I went to Sears and bought a walker for Dad. I helped him learn to walk with it, and then on crutches. Then eventually he was able to get by with just a cane. He gave up the cane too. His injury brought about a change in the job safety laws in Pennsylvania. They had to give him a job when he was finally able to return to work, and they put him on the security gate as a guard. After Dad got hurt he was only getting $19.00 a week. We were living in the projects in the Richard Allen Homes then. The rent was reduced to $19.00 a month and everything else had to be paid out of the little bit left over. There were vendors who came through the projects. The milk man, egg man and vegetable man used to give me credit and let me pay when I had some money, after they learned that Dad got hurt. I would send you kids to the vegetable man with a note and he would send me a lot more than he charged me for. Then every Saturday we used to go to the store with a little red wagon. The man in the store must have felt sorry for me with all you kids. Once he showed me some bent can goods in the back of the store and let me have them. I put the boxes of canned goods in the wagon with you small kids on top of them, as the older ones pulled it. One of the neighborhood drunks said, "Hey, lady, you sure got a lot of food there. It should last you a long time." Then my aunt Martha, who worked for Campbell's Soup, started giving us unlabeled cans. I don't know how I did it, but we always had something to eat and nothing was ever cut off.

AS RELATED BY FLORENCE

Henry Robinson was our paternal grandfather, and I don't remember my grandmother. There were three children, our father David Nathaniel, James, and Helen Robinson. David and I were born in Maryland, and Mom was only seventeen when she split with our father David Robinson, who died when we were young. We lived with Grandpa Charles Owens and Grandma Florence Owens in Windsor, Maryland, until Mom headed for Ambler, Pennsylvania, after uniting with John Dean. Dave didn't come to Ambler right away, staying in Maryland until he was around age nine or ten.

Then came the Great Depression, and things were really tough. There was no work for the men, and Poppa John couldn't find permanent work. He used to scavenge for coal and wood to heat the house. The women could sometimes pick up some day work, domestic work, in private homes. There was very little money, and nothing was ever wasted. We had to help out with the other ten children. By the time the Dean kids got shoes and clothes, there was nothing left for David and me. We never had much, but we had each other and have been a pretty close family. We lived in the same small house on Orange Avenue for all those years. Dave was the big brother and helped out as best he could. I think he taught all our brothers and sisters how to drive. He was a mentor for all of us. I admire what he did for everyone.

I thought Dave was too hard on you kids, the way he made you behave wherever you went. But I see that it really paid off.

PART I: FOUNDATIONAL YEARS

CHAPTER ONE

FAIRLY WELL, THANK YOU

There were five stair-step children born of the union of my Mom and Pop, Margaret Pauline Christopher and David Nathaniel Robinson. Sister Eleanor Marie was the first born on August 9, 1943. Next was David Nathaniel, Jr., born January 6, 1945; followed by Clarence Hamilton, born December 12, 1946. Wayne Barry was born February 14, 1948. Momma said that I arrived in a hurry after she went into labor because of Dad's insistence that they attend the Memorial Day parade. So on the afternoon of May 30, 1949, in Abington Pennsylvania, just outside of Philadelphia, I forced my entry into the world, perhaps because of the rhythm of the music. Although I was the subject of the launching, I don't recollect the event, and must defer to Momma's version of it. After my birth, Momma got fixed so she wouldn't have any more children. I don't know if I was the cause of that decision because of my big head, or Momma felt she had done enough for motherhood. Or maybe my folks felt they had finally got it right with my birth. Anyway being the last in line had some advantages, such as learning what not to do from my senior siblings, and getting my brothers' hand-me-downs. Being a Memorial Day baby may account for my patriotic genes, which I will get to later. Thus Memorial Days are always special to me.

I am impressed by the generation of Americans who endured the Great Depression and saved the world during World War II, thus etching a new template of opportunity for those who choose to participate in the game of upward mobility in our society. I am of the stock of hardy people initially tied to the soil of the American South. One distinguishing feature they shared is their willingness to do a day's work. "Day work" was the common vocational vernacular for women of color who did domestic work. It was a form of entrepreneurship by which one could work in multiple venues during the week and not be controlled by one master. From that backdrop, many business opportunities developed. For example, two of my great aunts, Marie and Emma Johnson, forged their way from the tobacco fields of rural Brunswick County, Virginia, in the early twentieth century to work for well-off white families in the Philadelphia area. Attentive to their surroundings, the ladies absorbed and duplicated the business principles surrounding them every day. They purchased their own homes and followed their wealthy families to the Jersey Shore during the summers. They purchased a boarding house close to their employers, and took in relatives working at the shore during the summers. In addition to operating a boarding house in Cape May, New Jersey, they also ran beauty salons, catering services, and provided meals for temporary domestic laborers and visitors. They were self-sufficient and established financial security for themselves as a result of their own efforts. They also served as a conduit of opportunity for their relatives and strangers alike.

One of the other Johnson Sisters was my grandmother Mary Etta (Elaine) Johnson Christopher, or Sis Mary to kinfolks, or Aunt Mary to white folks. You see, everyone got tagged with a nickname, as if their given name was a disguise. The early morning smells emanating from Sis Mary's kitchen were fantastic, especially the fresh-ground Eight O'Clock coffee brand from the A&P store. The old wood stove cooked up some of the most delicious meals known to country folks. Those delicious "you-got-to-go-to-work breakfasts," complete with fatback, ham, sausage, eggs, apples, fried potatoes, biscuits, and rolls, washed down with buttermilk fresh from the cow, had to last you all morning long in the tobacco fields. Grandma Mary, with the assistance of her daughters, loaded up the breakfast table before walking a mile or so up the road to do the same for her white family.

Whenever asked how she was doing, she always responded, "Fairly well, thank you." She was born right at the start of the twentieth century, in rural Brunswick County, Virginia. Brunswick stew being originally concocted in Virginia might explain why her stews and one-pot meals were so good. You never knew what was in them. You just ate them. Grandma Mary always worked hard, usually with more energy and vigor than young folks. She and my grandfather, John Jasper Christopher, or Bro Jack to kinfolks, or Uncle Jack to white folks, had twelve children, two of whom died in infancy. They settled in Nottoway County, Virginia, on a small farm, where they started raising their family. However, at the start of World War II their land was taken by the federal government under the rule of eminent domain to construct Camp Pickett for the Army. The government assisted with the move, but part of the journey resembled a small wagon train with the mules pulling their wagons to their new place of residence along Virginia State Route 307 some twenty some miles away. It was in that setting that the meaning of work was engraved into my spirit. It made some lasting impressions on me that would aid in my sojourn in the workplace. We learned a lot from the back seats of Dotty's (Daddy's) succession of Ford station wagons, mostly woodies and some plain. U.S. Highway 1 between Philadelphia and Richmond, Virginia, was one of our pathways to learning and adventure.

U.S. Route 1 is the same highway that transported countless southern black folks north to a more promising land of opportunity. Dad had migrated from Maryland at an early age with his mother and sister to Ambler, Pennsylvania, a small town just north of Philadelphia. He was the second oldest of twelve children. My first recollection of my Dad was a glimpse of him in the hospital. I vaguely recall being with Mom as a toddler, entering a very bright room where everything was white with some undistinguishable figures moving around. We stopped at a bed and stood over the figure lying there. It was Dad, who on December 21, 1951, was torn apart in an accident at work. He was caught between two ceiling cranes which operated on parallel tracks like trains do on the ground. His leg, hip, and arm were broken, his stomach torn open, and his guts pulled out. Dad died but came back to life several times. One doctor told him he would be an invalid. But he knew otherwise. He was told he would never be able to walk, but he got his legs to work and started walking again. He had to work. He had to provide for his family. That is what fathers must do.

Mom migrated to Philadelphia shortly before World War II. She did domestic work, or day work as folks called it, which was a traditional occupation for young women with little education or no occupational skills. Mom introduced me to day work at an early age, because I had to accompany her to clean houses before I was old enough to attend school. She swears that scrubbing all those kitchen floors on her knees wore her knees out. The last chore of the day work ritual was waxing the kitchen floor with Johnson paste wax as we left through the rear door. Day work was ideal for a hungry, curious child. Refrigerators were well stocked with real lunch meat and cold Pepsi. Sometimes there were kids in the neighborhood to play with. The fringe benefits included receiving stuff from the homeowners, such as clothing their children had outgrown, and old magazines. I loved the variety of magazines and was captivated by the pictures in *Time, Look,* and *National Geographic.* I would race through my designated duties of vacuuming and dusting so I could look at magazines or go play until it was time to leave. Browsing through the magazines was like traveling through the world. I was introduced to brand-new places, and intrigued by them. I imagined that someday I might travel through the world and see those intriguing places. There were occupational hazards with day work, though. Hurricane Hazel caught Mom and me at the bus stop, and it felt like we were going to be blown away. We hugged the telephone pole until the bus finally arrived and took us to the subway. We got back to the protection of the cinder block walls of the projects just in time.

Once I started Spring Garden Elementary School, Mom was on her own. However, when school was out I would still accompany her to work to help her out. Eventually I was picking up small side jobs of my own, like washing windows and raking leaves. I vividly remember meeting a couple where the husband had lost his job. Of significance to me was that this seemingly old man, actually middle aged, was in school trying to be retrained in a new field. I played with his slide rule but didn't know what it was for. I became convinced that there is no such thing as job security, and that we should be prepared for the unexpected in life. In particular, we should prepare ourselves with multiple skills and never indulge in self-pity if our present livelihood evaporates or becomes reduced. I developed a work ethic of one day at a time. I felt that acquiring additional skills would be like adding to a wardrobe. Instead of discarding anything, I would just add more to the existing inventory. More skills would add extra security and more options.

Dad's station wagons continued to take us to all sorts of places and to serve others in need of transportation. We all piled in the station wagon to go grocery shopping, and would race down the narrow aisles of the A&P store getting what Mom told us to get. There was telephone book delivery, newspaper delivery, Boy Scout activities, sightseeing, and trips to the park. Southeastern Pennsylvania offered a wealth of cultural and recreational opportunities, including museums, historical sites, parks and public events. A favorite was the drive-in theater, charging a dollar per car load. Dad kept life interesting, and often without notice we were in the car with a picnic basket, a jug of Kool-Aid, and cookies, heading off to places unknown. Most events were spontaneous, and we simply rode to where Dad was taking us, inventing games to play along the way, such as counting the number of cars of a particular make, or "mine," where the first to see and claim an item could claim ownership of it. I won a lot of nice cars and houses along the way. Dad liked to visit friends and family, and during these visits he required us to behave. This insistence of Dad's on good behavior was a training ground for discipline and patience. Children have to be trained in all aspects of behavior and learn how to be still. It doesn't come naturally.

December 21, 1955, marked a significant day for the Robinson Family. It was moving day from the Richard Allen Housing Projects in the Spring Garden section of Philadelphia to a row house near Germantown in the northwest section of town. It was good-bye projects,

Jessup Place and Brown Place, and hello to 5929 North 21st Street. Ours was a typical three bedroom, one bath row house built in the earlier part of the century. The boys were stacked in four Army surplus metal bunk beds in the rear bedroom and Sister Eleanor had the small middle room to herself. Mom and Dad had the front bedroom. This move was different from our last move, from one section of the projects to another, after Dad was injured and a first floor unit became available. For that move we used a push cart to move our stuff. This time the Ford wagon towed a small U-Haul trailer. In only two trips we moved all our worldly possessions, and then hurriedly unloaded the trailer so the neighbors wouldn't get a glimpse of our tattered possessions.

Our first meal in our new home came from the local corner store: a loaf of soft white bread downed by sparkling tap water. To our growling bellies it was a king's feast. We used the natural refrigeration of the cold winter air to preserve our perishables on the back stoop until my folks could muster up the down payment for a refrigerator from Sears. When Christmas Eve arrived Dad took his paycheck and stretched it as far as he could. We hit the Farmers Market for food items, got a few gifts and found a free Christmas tree, all in the space of a few hours before settling down to decorating and cooking. Though our skinny tree was mostly bare, with little underneath it, Mom's rolls and the turkey and trimmings made it a great Christmas. In those days people lived within their means, and when they ran out of money and provisions, they went without until the next payday.

The house rules were simple. You did what you were told to do, and your immediate response was required. We pitched in to do the household chores. We were all trained to cook, sew, clean, wash, and iron. "I don't know how" was unacceptable. Mom did the major cooking, because food was too precious to waste. Then we took turns cooking depending on our activities. Dad pitched in occasionally to whip up some mashed potatoes or potato salad, but we shied away from his cooking, owing to past experience when he served as our chef in the projects. Saturdays meant washing clothes in the old wringer washer and running them through the two rinsing tubs before hanging them on the outside clothesline. Then each of us was responsible for ironing our own clothes. Privileges did not begin until work ended. Cleaning the house and getting the clothes done were prerequisites for playing outside. And because Dad worked a half day on Saturday everything had to be done before he arrived home if we wanted to play outside. A spy was posted to announce when Dad arrived home. The cry "Dotty is here!" was the final warning to get everything wrapped up.

Ours was a super-sized extended family, with aunts, uncles, cousins, and helpful neighbors close by. If there was a need, somebody would step in to help. Great Aunt Martha worked for

Campbell Soup Company, where the workers were given the unlabeled canned goods. Martha collected the cans and gave them to us. So we had mystery meals. We would enthusiastically open a can and hope for the best. Would it be the grand prize of chicken noodle soup, or the dreaded split pea soup? We ate whatever was in the can and usually had bread for a government cheese sandwich to complement it. Actually we were accustomed to mystery meals because Dad was our cook in the projects after he came home from the hospital. Mom at that time had to work to feed us. Dad's food preparation philosophy was that what we did not eat for one meal would be the basic item for the subsequent meal. The menu was an unpredictable collage of food groups. The delicacies included mashed potatoes or oatmeal garnished with green peas, surplus food extravaganza, and other undesirable combinations now removed from memory. We never could get all the lumps out of the powdered milk. And the powdered eggs rivaled anything the worst Army cook could whip up. There was always something to eat, although it was seldom what we wanted. The exceptions were Sundays and holidays, when there were identifiable separate entrees such as chicken, ham, mashed potatoes, rice, green peas, string beans, and corn. Relief came with the annual trips to Virginia when we would return with a carload of fruits and vegetables.

My earliest recollection of our Virginia trips was being in the projects and packing up the old Dodge, which predated the Ford wagons, the night school let out, and heading south in the dark of the night to get us out of the urban jungle for the summer. Dad liked to drive at night, I guess to keep us asleep and to avoid the obligatory, "I gotta use the bathroom," or "Are we there yet?" The traffic was usually light, with just trucks. Dad felt comfortable around truckers, having been a truck driver during World War II. The 325 mile trip took about eight hours along U.S. Highway 1 south, thence U.S. Highway 360 west, before the interstate highways opened up. We would sleep through the night and wake up with the rising sun silhouetting the red roof of Grandpa Jack's barn. "We're here, we're here," would arouse any remaining sleepers. We were ready to eat once we exited the car. And eat we did.

Those summer trips were particularly meaningful regarding day work. As a young lad I drew light duty. I filled the wood box for the cook stove, collected fallen fruit, and gathered eggs. Being too young to tote water from the well to the house or work in the fields allowed a lot of time for mischief like throwing apples at the hogs and chasing chickens. As I got older, the summer work intensified. The tobacco fields required serious labor. The tobacco plants, which were maturing when we arrived in late June, had to be watered, and suckers (flowering weeds) had to be pulled off the plants. We had to go with Grandpa and our uncles on the mule-drawn wagon to the creek to fill barrels with water for the plants. We would form a bucket line to scoop water into the buckets and pass it to be dumped into 55 gallon drums.

Once filled, the drums were covered with burlap bags to minimize sloshing as we made our way to the fields to water the plants by hand. By late summer the leaves were ready to be pulled and hung in the tobacco barns to dry. This was a community effort, with families rotating among farms to help one another get the crops in. Paid labor was unheard of then. Your paycheck was a hearty meal.

The days were usually divided into morning and evening work, with midday yielding to some serious eating. The meals that came from Grandma's stove were plain but filling. She knew how to put anything in a pot and make a meal out of it. Cooking and sewing were her passions. She would take old material destined for the rag bag or burn barrel and make beautiful quilts that kept us warm in the winter. Her quilts were a patchwork of oddities, wherein the various materials and designs blended to form a unique artistic production. Pieces of elegant material were sewn alongside flannel, contrasting stripes and plaids were patched together, and the hand stitching holding the pieces together was tied and knotted on the back, with smooth artistry up front. Thinking of Grandma's quilts remind me of our nation's diverse heritage, wherein the rich and poor, educated and unsophisticated, refined and rough, are bonded together in quilt-like fashion. Each patch carries equal importance and the mosaic forms the core of America. We are a collection of colors, cultures, languages, and religions blended together.

There was one ritual never to be interfered with: Grandma's noontime soap operas. Silence was commanded as she sat in front of the cloudy TV screen fussing at the actors on *The Edge of Night* and *Search for Tomorrow*. Mary Christopher was physically active nearly all of her life, despite the diabetes she controlled with insulin and walking, until Alzheimer's kicked in to rob her of her health. She lived an active 89 years, with all but her last few years being fairly well, thank you.

CHAPTER TWO

GROWING UP PHILLY

Right after Labor Day the Ford station wagon would arrive to round us up and return to Philadelphia with a full complement of fruits, vegetables, and smoked meat. The luggage carrier on the car roof housed our meager baggage, while the perishables shared space with us inside the vehicle. The first few days back in Philly were devoted to shucking, hulling, peeling, and canning vegetables. The shelves in the basement were then well stocked with jars of fruits and vegetables. Applesauce was a main staple. Applesauce with cinnamon and toast was a household staple.

The kids in rural Virginia returned to school in mid-August, before we would return to Philadelphia. I was saddened by the low quality of education offered black children. There was a one-room schoolhouse right across the road from my grandparents for grades one through seven. The community helped to construct it, because there would have been no school. Local families had to sponsor a schoolteacher. A teacher named Miss Perry occupied the best room in my grandparents' crowded home, which left two other bedrooms for their several children still at home. Meanwhile in Philly the quality of education was determined by location. The schools in our new neighborhood were superior to those in the Spring Garden area. We entered Joseph Pennell Elementary School and were introduced to a more intense learning environment. The school day was split into two parts, morning and afternoon. At lunchtime the children marched home to eat, and returned an hour later to resume class. Our faces were well known to our teachers, leaving little opportunity to misbehave. The word of any infractions would trickle back home and there would be an appointment with Dotty's big black belt. I stepped boldly into a new academic environment, and discovered that school was work in a different package. In addition to the classroom stuff there were chores assigned to each student. My favorite was cleaning the chalkboard erasers which entailed going out on the fire escape and clapping the erasers together to remove the chalk. This exciting task was surpassed only by membership in the Safety Patrol, which assisted the crossing guards and the members wore a distinctive belt and displayed a badge of authority.

One of my favorite routes home from school took me through an alley featuring a mean dog. The fence housing the dog was a barrier begging to be breached. One day, as the result of a dare, I climbed over the fence and challenged the canine. But having miscalculated the number of steps back to the fence, my final leap came up short. I left part of my pants in the dog's mouth and ran home trying to fabricate an excuse for the damage. The destruction of my school clothes was not a small matter because we only got one set at the beginning of the school year, and it had to last. Because I was usually the one who retired the hand-me-down clothes I managed to escape my mother's wrath. On another occasion, while doing some tree adventurism I lost my footing and wound up on the concrete, head first. Mom always said we had hard heads. After the experience of my sister cleaning the wound with a whole bottle of Listerine, I gave up tree climbing.

After elementary school we headed to Wagner Junior High School. The daily walk covered about 12 blocks. Junior high school, consisting of grades seven, eight, and nine, was managed chaos. It meant home rooms and changing classes. These were the in-between years, when voices and anatomies change. There was no more afternoon strolls home for lunch. Lunch was from the cafeteria or brown bags. For us it was brown bags with whatever sandwich ingredients were available, usually bologna and cheese, or peanut butter and jelly. The paper bag was neatly folded and taken back home to be used again. Junior high was also the beginning of controlled social interaction between girls and boys. Once a week in the gym there was a sock hop. For a small fee one could hold up the walls watching others dance or actually dance under the watchful eyes of a matriarch teacher. Junior high started the process of identifying and separating students by academic performance. Junior high school is where academic branding began. There were three main groupings – academic, vocational, and trade. I had no intention of wasting my free education. I had cousins in Prince Edward County, Virginia, who were denied the opportunity to go to school because the school board chose to shut the schools down rather than integrate them. I sought academic achievement so I could have some options. I also joined the school track team and the Boy Scouts.

Philadelphia decided to revert to a single year enrollment in the fall of each year. So those of us who had started school in the January enrollment period had to attend summer school to catch up to the fall enrollees. For me that meant graduating in June instead of January. In addition I caught up with my brother Wayne so we wound up in the same grade. We graduated from Wagner Junior High School in June 1963 decked out in our Sunday clothes, our wool suits, which were the bounty from Mom's day work for a family of tailors.

The last stop of my secondary education was Germantown High School located in historic Germantown along the stone-lined Germantown Avenue with trolley tracks in the center. The boundaries of the area served by the school were such that children from all backgrounds attended. It was a mixing bowl for children from well-to-do families and poor families. The curriculum was rigorous, and my lazy streak was exposed in tenth-grade biology. Biology was the last class of the day. The young teacher, fresh out of college, failed to challenge or inspire lazy students. His monotone voice and dry teaching style at the end of the day was uninspiring. He allowed his students to drift into mediocrity. (Around 2:30 p.m. November 22, 1963, we received word in his class that President Kennedy had been assassinated). Shock struck my academic standing when my laziness earned me the grade of D. Fortunately the next semester netted us a new teacher. Her elderly appearance belied her dynamic teaching style. She demanded our best effort, and soon identified the students who were slacking off. She would return our test papers in ascending order of our grades, from the lowest to the highest. I soon went from being one of the first to receive my test back to being the very last. I received an A and a valuable lesson. A good teacher motivates by any means necessary. Teachers who establish and enforce tough standards in the classroom make it clear to students that they must fall in line and do their best. Holding people strictly accountable for their conduct in the classroom, as well as in the home, and in the community, is the only way to establish and maintain a disciplined society.

As we grew in maturity we no longer spent summers in Virginia. We took advantage of programs offered by Philadelphia's Division of Parks and Recreation and began to participate in Boy Scout summer camp and take on summer jobs. One memorable summer I earned merit badges for the rank of Star Scout. One of the badges was for cycling. Dad had found me a beautiful bicycle with coaster brakes and an auxiliary hand brake. It was a middle-weight bike resembling the popular three-speed English Racer of that era. Dad had a knack for finding bargains and managed to buy each of us roller skates, hula hoops, bicycles, and the like. I rode my bike nearly everywhere. On one trip to the West Oak Lane Library I returned to the bicycle rack and found my bike missing. The thief had broken my cheap lock and made off with my most cherished possession. I was heartbroken but had learned a valuable lesson regarding securing one's property. I searched for my bike from block to block and combed the city storage and abandoned property sites to no avail. I had to retrieve one of the old fashion heavyweight bikes from the garage and make it roadworthy before heading off to cruise the roads of eastern Pennsylvania by pedal power for the cycling merit badge.

I did some trips with my riding buddy Steve Williams. Steve had a lightweight three-speed English Racer and I had a heavyweight fifty-pound dinosaur to push up and down the hills. I would build up speed going downhill which would give me a running start for the upcoming hill, and I would have to pump like crazy to make it to the top. On one long ride my brother Wayne decided to ride with us. We planned our route and had a great ride, sleeping under the stars in the parks. We were riding through the scenic Delaware River Valley in Bucks County, Pennsylvania, when a surprise downpour thoroughly drenched us. We had failed to fulfill the Boy Scout Motto of "Be Prepared." So as night fell on us we had to send an SOS to Mom. She arrived in her old Mercury, and we got into the car cold and shivering for the ride back home. Thank God for Moms.

Earning pocket money in the city was only limited by one's pride and imagination. All you had to do was look around and observe how people did their day work. Recycling, for example, has always been with us. There was the junk man who drove his battered pickup truck through the neighborhood collecting metal on the night before trash collection day. The rag man collected old clothing and cloth and the paper man searched for paper and cardboard. They were unglamorous in their old trucks or horse-drawn carts, but they made an honest living. We were also in the recycling business, primarily newspaper for the Scout troop. At times our garage would be a newspaper depository until there was enough to cash in. Dad took on telephone book delivery, which involved the kids riding on the tailgate, hopping off with the heavy books, dropping them on door steps, and then racing back to the car for more books. It was fun for us and turned into a competitive event.

My early day work ventures included cutting grass, washing cars, shoveling snow, and running errands for neighbors. Instead of charging my neighbors a set price, I accepted whatever payment they deemed appropriate. Sometimes I received payment in goods instead of money. The old man down the street, who had his hands full trying to take care of his mentally-retarded son, had me chop down a small jungle he called a yard. It was a neighborhood eyesore. I used a swing blade sickle as my weapon against the weeds. The stubborn weeds meant to defeat me, causing the handle to come off my swing blade. A neighbor observing from across the street came to my aid and fixed my weapon. My compensation for the job was soda bottles so old that roaches had taken up residence in them and died. It took a couple of washing with hot water to dislodge the critters before I could take the bottles to the corner store and exchange them for money. I got a nickel for the big ones and two cents for the little ones. I think I made a buck.

Snow was always welcomed because of its economic and recreational value, especially if school was canceled. After shoveling our sidewalk my next stop was the next street over to shovel Emma and Fannie Christopher's sidewalk. The sisters were my maternal great aunts. They worked in the homes of white families and needed to get to work regardless of the weather. I then headed out to the suburbs to start shoveling and work my way back. Because my preferred customers were about three miles out I dressed in layers and walked along the plowed streets.

As an early riser I was usually up and out before my competition could steal my customers. I had a few regulars whose sidewalks and driveways would be shoveled before I rang the doorbell to collect my money. There was often some hot chocolate or tea waiting for me. I couldn't tarry long as I backtracked toward home, shoveling my way back. I didn't care if I got wet or cold, because the old hot-water radiators were cranked up at home. I usually stopped by the local grocery store to grab a half gallon of fifty-cent vanilla ice cream and root beer or orange soda. My reward was to sit by the radiator and sip my root beer or orange floats. It was never too cold for ice cream floats. I had earned them.

In addition there were established businesses that took on periodic help. I tried my hand at a car wash as temporary help. The young kids were relegated to washing the inside windows of cars because the work was tedious and required a lot of stretching and contortions. I met the challenge of interior window washing the short time I stayed there. The car wash crew was a rare assembly of people, sometimes a bunch of derelict men and a few women. The men's locker room was a combination changing area, break area, lunch room, rest room, and storage area. The place was filled with generally unpleasant blended aromas. The tips from customers all went into a box to be split only by the regular workers.

I entered my junior year of high school in September 1964. The juniors had less pressure on them than the freshmen, who were trying to find their identity, and the seniors who were struggling to graduate. I decided to follow the industrial arts curriculum, which was a combination of academic work and the building trades. That way I would have all bases covered in case I didn't go to college. My goal was to be an engineer, but I was willing to settle for the building trades. I took all the math and science courses offered. So I attended algebra, geometry, trigonometry, chemistry, physics, English, and Spanish with the smart kids. Then I attended mechanical drawing, wood shop, metal shop, and electronics with the less academically gifted. Most of the guys were uninterested in school, and just marking time until they either graduated or dropped out. It was my observation that the brain outlasted the back, so I did everything in my power to prepare for college and exercise brain power.

When I started my research for college at the start of eleventh grade I soon realized that it would take more than grades to get into college. I therefore participated in extracurricular activities and was involved in the church and community. Even though I disliked distance running, I joined the cross-country team, which had no roster limits. The basketball coach used cross-country in the off-season to whip his basketball players into shape. Cross-country meets were held in Fairmont Park with hundreds of boys from all the high schools negotiating the 2.5 mile course in a test of stamina. Though I was never competitive, at least I was earning an athletic letter. Junior year seemed to be the key year for grades on college applications. So it was time to buckle down for schoolwork and prepare for the Scholastic Aptitude Test (SAT). At this time I reached my sixteenth birthday.

The significance of age sixteen in Pennsylvania is that it is the minimum age for a learner's permit, to be followed by the coveted driver's license, a teenager's most treasured possession. As with all of us kids, my Dad was my driving instructor, and I got to drive the station wagon. On my first try I flunked the driving proficiency part of the examination for a license, but returned to take and pass the test.

Once licensed, boys see themselves as young men in need of a car. I knew that the only way that I was going to have a car was to save my money and ask my Dad to look for one. I continued to walk to school to save the 85 cents carfare. As I earned money I had two bankers, the Pennsylvania Savings Fund Society (PFSF) and my Mom. All young people should honor their parents by contributing to the household financially, at least in some small way. My routine was to give Mom some money to keep in the event she needed something. She was a good banker and certainly knew how to conserve money.

Brother Wayne and I landed temporary jobs at a federally-funded summer jobs program during the summer of 1965. Each morning we walked to the Germantown Town Center with our brown bag lunch for a day's work. We mostly did beautification projects such as landscaping and painting. When my supervisor recognized my enthusiasm for work, I graduated to floor refinishing and was then asked to participate in an archeology project in the old Germantown Square. The archeological project was dirty and tedious. We carefully dug down a few inches, and then sifted the dirt through screens to trap artifacts. The project chief was a one-armed man with a safari hat, and his assistant, who resembled Miss. Hathaway in the *Beverly Hillbillies*

TV show, catalogued the artifacts. It was dirty, undignified, hot, and sweaty work, in full view of the curious public. I hoped no one who knew me would see me. After the government portion of the grant was exhausted we were asked to stay on for $1.25 an hour. My coworkers stood together to demand an increase for the backbreaking work. When their demand was rejected, they elected not to return to work. So much for organized labor, I thought. I stayed for the remaining few weeks before school started to earn as much as I could. This was, after all, not my life's work, just a means to help me earn money for college. By the end of the summer I had netted a few hundred dollars, some of which went for school clothes before the rest went into an account at PSFS.

Being thrifty is one of the Boy Scout Laws. Having a little money is dangerous for an undisciplined person. I began to have visions of cars and nice clothes. After all, cars are a symbol of freedom in America, and every young man is entitled to a car, at least in his imagination. Never mind the realities of maintenance, insurance, and gas. I felt there was a car in my future. I just didn't know when. In preparation of that moment I continued to walk everywhere to save money. I also used some of the money to take the SAT and send out college applications.

In my senior year I was accepted into the National Honor Society. Because I failed to prepare adequately for the SAT my test scores failed to reflect my abilities. I landed an after school job tutoring small children. Then I netted a job in a fish store, earning a dollar an hour. I always gave some money to Mom and saved the rest. The business was on 5th Street, a walk of over 20 blocks from home. An elderly Jewish couple owned the store, and Hattie was their long-term employee. She was the cook and I was her helper. Hattie had been a faithful worker for many years, but never made much money. She was grossly overweight and poor health and family problems had aged her beyond her years. Hattie prepared some excellent seafood and salads. I handled all the logistics, like peeling potatoes and preparing paper products for the orders. Mr. Fisher, the diminutive proprietor, drove me around to deliver orders. He cold barely see over the steering wheel of his car. There was a degree of hazardous duty as he drove his big Chevy like a frustrated New York taxi driver. At least I got to keep the tips from customers. I also got to eat for free. Again I saved money by eating at work and walking. So my college fund grew weekly by a few dollars.

The reality of financing college was sinking in. My meager savings would only be a drop in the bucket. Therefore I pondered the opportunities derived from military service and carefully reviewed information I received from the service academies. I'd been exposed to the Army, having two uncles who were career soldiers and a brother, David, who was an NCO. Brother

Clarence had joined the Marine Corp, making military service look like a definite option. I decided to seek admission to the United States Military Academy and the Coast Guard Academy. I wrote to my United States Senators and Congressman requesting consideration for an appointment. Though I failed to receive an appointment, my Congressman, the Honorable William Green, allowed my name to be placed into the pool of alternate candidates, which meant that I could be evaluated for an unanticipated vacancy.

In the spring of 1966 I received a letter directing me to take a physical examination at the United States Army Hospital at Valley Forge, Pennsylvania. Dad deposited me there for a few days of testing. The medical staff checked every part of my body, and explored everywhere there was an opening. I also took a physical fitness test to measure strength, endurance, and agility. Somehow I miscalculated my laps during the shuttle run and had to run it twice. This was shortly after lunch. I displayed good speed but lost my lunch in the process. Dad returned to pick me up at the conclusion of the tests. I was thankful for the opportunity to compete. Going to college was going to be a great privilege. There was only one college graduate in all the generations of paternal and maternal kinsmen, and that was my aunt Mary Elaine Christopher. She was slightly older than my sister, and worked her way through Virginia State College by spending her summers in Philadelphia and Cape May cleaning hotel rooms. I knew that if Elaine could do it, so could I. My options were attending the local campus of Pennsylvania State University or a service academy. Dad knew I wanted a car and had saved diligently. With fifty dollars of my money he found me my first car. It was a four door green 1955 Ford Fairlane, which required generous portions of oil along with gas. It was an ugly duckling, but I had arrived at the pinnacle of American teenagerism. I had wheels. I had freedom. I knew about preventive maintenance from my dad and lifted the hood regularly to check on the life blood of my vehicle. It allowed me to expand my business ventures, such as washing windows and light painting in the suburbs.

I went about senior year activities such as the senior prom and our class trip without much thought about acceptance to college. I was set to attend college locally since I had my car. The class trip was to Bear Mountain, New York. We rode a bus from Philly to New York City and had a boat ride up the Hudson River to Bear Mountain. I was in the home stretch right before graduation when I received an acceptance letter for admission to the United States Coast Guard Academy, New London, Connecticut. After locating New London on a map, I accepted the invitation and mailed off the obligatory deposit. Shortly thereafter I received a letter of acceptance to the United States Military Academy, West Point, New York. After some deep thought I decided to withdraw my acceptance to the Coast Guard Academy and headed for West Point.

PART III: SOLDIERING

CHAPTER THREE

THE DAYS

I reported to the United States Military Academy, West Point, New York, on July 1, 1966, a mere two weeks after high school graduation. Dad volunteered to drive me there. Mom, Dad, and I left early for the 150-mile trip on a beautiful July 1st. I had never visited West Point, though I'd come close while on the class trip to Bear Mountain. The Pennsylvania Turnpike intersected with the infamous New Jersey Turnpike, with its array of disgusting smells in Northern Jersey. We stopped at the Howard Johnson Restaurant on the turnpike for breakfast. I was too nervous to take more than a few bites out of my pancakes. We pulled onto Highway 9W at Fort Lee, New Jersey, and cruised along the West Bank of the picturesque Hudson River, viewing the New York skyline and passing through small towns, and then driving by the Merchant Marine Academy. Then we went through the Bear Mountain traffic circle and the town of Highland Falls, before entering the main gate of the United States Military Academy.

My first impression was that West Point looked like a nice place. I exited my parents' car with my shaving kit and marched off. I was directed to the gym and placed in PT shorts, a white T-shirt and black oxford shoes, and tagged. Everything was well choreographed and thus began the transformation of over 1,100 civilians into new cadets. This was Reception Day for new cadets, raw meat for the upperclassmen. If a plebe is the lowest form of human existence, a new cadet is lower. New cadets were fresh bait for upperclassmen, juniors and seniors, who were given charge over the newbees during the process of soldierization, or turning civilians into soldiers.

Reporting to the man in the red sash transformed my life. He was in my face screaming and barking orders. I started to question my sanity and the decision to enter the Academy. The tags we wore had to be signed at various stations. Though I had a fresh skinhead haircut, I had to sit in the barber's chair and let the barber touch my head with his clippers so he could check the haircut box. Military lesson number one is to obey orders and not look for logic. At the uniform station a tailored uniform awaited me, and with minor alterations I was ready to move on to other stations. After collecting several duffel bags of gear, I and the other new cadets were escorted to our barracks.

New Cadet Training, dubbed "Beast Barracks," was in the cadet area quadrangle dating back more than a century. Personal items such as underwear and hygiene items were laid out on our bunks. After dropping our bags we were drilled in marching in the quadrangle in preparation for the swearing in ceremony at Trophy Point, a postcard perfect setting at the bend of the Hudson River. A regiment of skinhead new cadets dressed in white shirts and gray pants marched before the pressing crowd of proud family and friends to be inducted into the United States Army. There were seven cadets of color among the more than eleven hundred inductees. They were Robert Cousar from Pittsburgh, Roderick Morgan from Indianapolis, Robert Mason from Washington, D.C., Willie Price from Chicago, Trevor Reid from the Bronx, Kenneth Thomas from Biloxi, and me. We would all graduate together four years later.

Soon the reality of my decision to attend West Point started to set in. There is the right way to do things, the wrong way, the Army way and the West Point way. We were quickly introduced to the West Point way. For example, eating involved more than just gulping down food. Bracing was required. A plebe had to sit erect on the front part of his chair, back straight, eyes straight, neck back. Food had to be taken in small bites and consumed without looking down. The result was a "square meal" of bringing food up from the plate to eye level, then over to the mouth. Permission was required to use ice cubes in your beverage or make a sandwich. We sat ten to a table, eight plebes and two upperclassmen, and plebes had table duties, including serving upperclassmen their beverages and desserts. The mess hall was a mammoth place capable of seating about four thousand cadets. Food was stored in carts and served family style. The whole place could be fed in about 20 minutes. Our first few meals were merely ceremonial, as we were taught table manners and ran out of time for eating. The leftover food, essentially all of it, was unceremoniously scraped into the garbage as we were hustled to the next training event. I suspect the pigs on New Jersey's hog farms were well fed.

As hunger pains set in I reminisced about those uneaten golden brown pancakes I'd left on my plate at the Howard Johnson. Food fantasies filled our minds as our bellies growled.

Beast Barracks was Army boot camp. Training included physical fitness, drill and ceremonies, marksmanship, weapons, military courtesy and history, individual combat tactics, small unit movements, first aid, and chemical defense, which culminated in a bivouac. To add to the stress there was West Point lore contained in "Bugle Notes," dubbed the Plebe Bible. This had to be memorized along with The Days, the numerical countdown to significant events such as football games, holidays, Christmas break, and graduation. Whenever asked, a plebe would respond with, "Sir. The Days....!", and then recite the number of days remaining before each significant event. The plebes were unaware of the value of the agonizing ritual in training the mind to retain and manage bits of information. Everyone was subjected to the same treatment, be he the son of a general or a janitor. The cadre consisted of junior and senior cadets, who served as drill sergeants. They trained and kept watch over the flock of new cadets under the supervision of Army officers assigned as tactical officers. The cadet cadre had carte blanche to play whatever games they desired, save physical hazing. We were housed in the nineteenth-century gray barracks arranged in a quadrangle facing a central courtyard. Old soldiers like Bradley, MacArthur, Patton, and Eisenhower had lived there. Three floors of two man rooms were in each stairwell. The stairwells were connected by the basement, which housed the toilets and showers.

In the wee morning hours, fit only for roosters and dairy farmers, we were awakened by the "Hellcats," a drum and bugle ensemble. Day Two had arrived. This day consisted of physical training (PT), an instant shower, breakfast food sighting, training, lunch food sighting, training, retreat, dinner food sighting, classes, uniform and equipment maintenance, and mandatory letters to your parents and the Congressman who had nominated you, followed by lights out to growling bellies. The Academy's philosophy was to reduce everyone to the same common denominator physically and mentally, and then to rebuild them. Trimming body fat while physically strengthening the body was one tactic used. Beast Barracks was famous for weight loss. Even my small 125-pound frame with little body fat was soon reduced to around 119 pounds. Our bodies survived off stored fat, as tons of food was trucked out for the pigs. As time marched on we were allowed to eat a little more but not enough to kill the hunger pains. One survival tactic was to sneak big bites and eat fast when the cadre didn't appear to be looking. Getting caught meant having to recite The Days and half the Bugle Notes. I couldn't understand why full rations were prepared only to be thrown away. Food was always on my mind, and I even reminisced about some of Dad's mystery meals. At least they had kept us alive. Subsequent days were the same. Religious affiliation was mandatory.

The Protestants marched to Trophy Point for Sunday services. Only religious services were off limits to harassment by upperclassmen. Otherwise harassment was a constant. It was mostly verbal, but no subject or language was taboo. One Sunday morning, decked out in the prescribed uniform, Cadet Whites, a white starched uniform, I was the first plebe to arrive in the formation area. I had failed to realize that it was a bad idea to be the only guy in formation because one might draw a crowd of upperclassmen. Obviously the flat-ass white boys were unused to the thick buttocks and spinal curvature of the Negroid anatomy.

"What is this, Mister? You look like shit," they shouted. "Repair yourself, smack head! Pull your butt in! Squeeze your cheeks like you're holding a dime." I inhaled, held my breath, drew my stomach in, and squeezed the cheeks of my buttocks as tight as I could, and stood as erect as a light pole. By then other plebes had arrived and absorbed some of the attention that had been focused on me. Anyway, it was the last time I was first to a formation. Too bad those guys were ignorant of diversified asses. Uniformity and conformity are valued at West Point and, unfortunately, with the very low minority representation at that time, and with most white cadets coming from sterile white communities, they lacked exposure to people who didn't look like them. Even the Academy tried to reshape one's body with bracing (erect posture and holding neck back) to straighten the neck and back line. I even attempted to repair the curvature in my back and reduce my protruding buttocks with daily exercises consisting of lying on my back and attempting to drive my spine into the floor. It didn't work.

By the end of Beast Barracks we were a lot leaner, stronger, and meaner as a result of all the physical exercise and running everywhere. Beast Barracks ended with the return of all the cadets to the Academy. As we advanced from new cadets to plebes we were outnumbered three to one by the other cadets. This meant more eyes on us and more tormentors. The new sophomores, called yearlings, harbored fresh memories of plebeian life and were ready in their turn to exact some pain on the new flock of plebes. There were four regiments of cadets. I was assigned to Company E, First Regiment, or Company E-1. Company F-1 held the reputation as the Corps' meanest company. Plebes would rather walk through Hell than F-1 territory, where they were subject to being ambushed and severely harassed by the plebe-eating upperclassmen. Also assigned to F-1 was Benny Robinson, Class of 1968, a black cadet from California. He delighted in harassing plebes. Some claimed we looked alike, which caused me grief from some yearlings who, having received some of Benny's wrath as plebes, and assuming we were related, wanted to reciprocate. Hazing is an environmentally-induced addiction like alcoholism and wife beating. The addictions to which people are exposed tend to mold their actions regardless of all their promises to themselves and others to avoid such behavior in their own lives.

"Bugle Notes" contained much information that was required knowledge for plebes, and its contents were the subject of interrogation by upperclassmen. In addition, plebes had to know the daily menu, movie schedule, football schedule, and, of course, The Days. So one's mind was always cluttered with insignificant data. All of this information, known as poop, was at the immediate disposal of any inquiring upperclassman. A plebe could find himself, surrounded by a group of upperclassmen, spouting off data for extended periods of time. Plebes were also assigned duties such as laundry delivery, mail delivery, guard duty, and minute calling – a countdown to formations. "Sir, there are five minutes remaining until the breakfast formation…." Plebes had to be in formation early to be inspected by the upperclassmen. As the academic year progressed, upperclassmen wasted less energy on the harassment of plebes, unless one stirred up someone's wrath. Plebes were able to socialize at home football games and Saturday night dances in Cullum Hall, the plebe meeting place. We had received formal dancing instruction in the same place earlier during the summer, as guys had to dance with each other under instruction for the waltz, fox trot, and other fancy footwork. Girls were bused in from surrounding schools on Saturday nights for the dances, or mixers, as they were called.

The Academy operated under the whole man concept, the development of the body, mind and soul. The academic curriculum was set. Everyone took the same courses and the same tests. Everyone competed in athletics and attended religious services. The recognized religious categories were Protestant, Catholic, and Jewish. I was Protestant and therefore made the long climb up the steep hill on Sunday mornings to the Cadet Chapel, with its imposing view of the grounds. Athletics consisted of competing in either intercollegiate or intramural sports.

We had taken diagnostic tests during Beast Barracks. As a result of my performance I was required to take a speed reading course to improve my reading comprehension. This course was taken after the regular classes. Academic deficiencies were the leading cause of attrition for cadets. It was an all or nothing system whereby cadets had to pass all subjects or be expelled. There were some unique cases in which a cadet could be turned back and return for a fifth year. Cadets had to be prepared for every class every day and were subject to grading each day. The small classes were rearranged periodically to group students by ability. I was assigned to the slower academic groups and the last group in calculus. That was the killer subject. It was a 7.5-hour course, with class held six days a week. Our first instruction was on the slide rule, that dinosaur manual calculator predating today's hand-held calculator. The calculus text consisted of manuals written by an Army Colonel who had been at West Point for a millennium. One familiar line in the test book was, "Now it is obvious to the casual observer…" I apparently was not a good observer because I fell into deep trouble in calculus. Actually it was not a case of lack of ability, but of fatigue.

The ultimate challenge in the life of a cadet was how to accomplish more in a day's work than there was time in the day. The typical day went from 0600 hours to 2200 hours. Plebes were unable to lie down or rest in between those times. The Academy forbade radios, televisions, and comfort items the first semester in an attempt to instill good study habits. My days took on the additional burdens of speed reading and remedial swimming. My intramural assignments were outdoor track, boxing, and cross-country. Plebes did not choose their sports. Remedial swimming occupied my other physically active time. Swimming is the best form of aerobic exercise because it utilizes all the muscles of the body. It is also physically taxing. The weekends were also swimming days. I was a prisoner of the pool, which I shared on weekends with children dashing about like little fish and mermaids. It was embarrassing. I was unable even to tread water or float. Survival swimming was part of the physical education curriculum and a requirement for graduation. The non-swimmers were dubbed the rock squad. Our classes began with the basics – breathing, kicking, stroking, then all three together; treading water; and self-flotation. Then it was sinking to the bottom of the pool and pushing off the bottom to break the surface and grab some air before repeating the process of walking underwater dubbed "bob and travel" – to traverse the water while fully clothed, and wearing a backpack filled with bricks. Also there were a required twenty-five-meter underwater swim, three meter platform blindfolded entry with clothing and with equipment, and fifteen-meter high-level entry from the roof rafters.

My body was not designed for swimming. It was more like the Titanic, and sought the water's bottom. It wasn't my fault that I was non-buoyant and sank like a rock. But my body composition did not count. My instructions were "Robinson, keep stroking." Instructors stayed dry. They were observers of plebes even in times of distress, but usually didn't move to assist anyone. Only once, when a swimmer was in trouble and rescue attempts by others had failed, did an instructor jump into the pool. I flunked swimming, and was thereafter assigned to remedial swimming, the "rock squad," until I was able to meet the standards. Lt. Parker, who was probably a former college swimming star working off his ROTC obligation, supervised remedial swimming. I spent many afternoons under his watch.

The extensive physical activity wore me out, impeding my ability to study. I was so lost in Calculus 101 class one day that I was summoned into my Tactical Officer's office and ordered to mandatory tutoring. I was to report to a junior from New York named Victor Garcia, Class of 1968. He was a serious, no nonsense kind of guy who was also the intramural heavyweight boxing champion, and assigned to the infamous Company F-1. I would report to Mr. Garcia each evening fearing for my life. The only way to escape this predicament was to pass Calculus 101. Christmas leave was coming, and unless I passed calculus I would not be returning to the Academy. Under the intimidation of Victor Garcia and the prospect of a very short college career, I opted to study hard and get my act together. I was down, but not out, going into the final exam. I finally realized that passing the course was not about understanding the material but learning a bunch of principles and applying them. I passed the final exam and passed Calculus 101. First semester plebe year was a success, thanks largely to programmed learning techniques such as the forced memorization of "Bugle Notes." From then on I promised myself that I would stay alert in class and grab all the information disseminated, because that was usually enough at least to pass the courses. I vowed not to be shy about seeking help. I was never in serious academic trouble again. Lessons learned: Pay attention, master the fundamentals, and seek help early and often. Instructors can program you for success, but you must put forth the effort. People are placed along our paths to help us. It is often the external forces that motivate and move us from mediocrity to merit. Helpers who are able to recognize our potential and propel us beyond our limitations to greater heights are dispatched around us. They can energize our untapped abilities and transform potential into accomplishment. But we must take advantage of the gift.

Plebe year meant confinement to the Academy grounds. We did leave as part of the Corps of Cadets to attend a few football games, and were given leave for Christmas. West Point is a cold, bleak place from Christmas until spring. I was still swimming under the watchful eyes of Lt. Parker. I often resembled a snowman after the chlorine and brisk winter air left my skin dry and ashy until I could get some lotion. I was detailed to intramural boxing that winter and cross-county in the spring. The cross-country course took a steady rise above the post, with us running uphill for half the course and downhill the other half.

The Spring break was the only time plebes were left unsupervised by upperclassmen. While the upperclassmen were away, plebes got to run the place, and their families were allowed to visit them. As the days began to wind down, The Days became easier to recite. The week preceding graduation was June Week, filled with pomp and circumstance. One of the parades ended with the recognition of the plebes. This was the rite of passage into being a full-fledged cadet. It was like the bar mitzvah or the debutante ball of cadet life. This marked the end of bracing and "square meals" and the other foolishness. Upon the graduation of the seniors of the Class of 1967 we advanced to the status of sophomores, or yearlings. We had a month off and then had to report to Camp Buckner for summer training.

I signed up for an exchange with the Coast Guard Academy. I made my way to New London, Connecticut, and joined the cadets on the USS Eagle, a tall ship and training vessel for the Coast Guard Academy. We set sail up the Atlantic Ocean and into the St. Lawrence River, and on to Montreal, Canada. Like my peers, I was assigned duties including standing watch, working in the engine room, and working the sails which meant climbing 50 to 100 feet up the masts and hanging out over the deck or the water. Quarters were cramped and served multiple purposes. The deck for sleeping was also the exercise area and the place for recreation. One day one of the cadets eating with me was asked by a peer to take his tray to the galley along with his. His response was, "What do you think I am, your nigger?" After two weeks at sea I was thankful that I had not elected to become a sailor. The sea is boring and spooky. Because the cruise was a training mission, the trip took five times longer than necessary. We cruised into the site of the Montreal Expo and lined the deck wearing our white uniforms. This was the end of the line for me. The cruise was a good experience and satisfied my curiosity about the sea.

After exploring the beautiful city of Montreal for a few days I was ready to leave for Philadelphia, but found that I was low on cash and the Canadians refused to cash American checks. I purchased a ticket for as far as my money would carry me. I wound up in Plattsburgh, New York, at night and out of money. I was saved by an NCO from the Air Force base who came to the bus station to pick up some luggage that had been lost. I asked for a ride to the airbase and explained my predicament to him. He cashed a check for me and I continued on my way to Philadelphia.

In Philadelphia I found that my old friends had scattered after high school. Those of my old friends who were still around seemed to have different interests from mine. While away I had matured faster than they had. Soon it was time to report to Camp Buckner. This camp was for tactical training in the woods, far removed from the prim and proper setting of the academic part of the military reservation. There were barracks, training areas, a mess hall by the lake, and many recreational activities. The training was an introduction to the combat arms, small unit tactics, and extensive physical conditioning. Member of the 82nd Airborne Division and other elite units were our instructors and senior cadets were the cadre. This was the military without textbooks or fancy parades. It was designed to test our ability to work together as a team, develop leadership skills, and increase our knowledge of how the Army operates. By the end of the summer we were in the best physical condition of our lives. Upon graduation we would be commissioned in on of the combat arms – infantry, armor, engineer, artillery, or signal. Camp Buckner would give us a chance to take a closer look at these career opportunities. This was typical Army training, physical training, breakfast, training, lunch, training, maintenance, dinner, maintenance, and lights out. The airborne troopers were fascinating to listen to and usually started their instruction with jokes and taught in spicy, profanity-laden language. Many were Vietnam veterans. They attempted to keep us alert and interested in the subject matter. Most training was hands-on. We would first get the instruction and then perform practical exercises. In the Army you are told what you are going to do, then you do it, and then you reinforce what you did – three whacks at the same stuff for the slow learners.

At Camp Buckner Saturday afternoons and Sundays after church constituted free time. We were forbidden to leave the camp but were allowed guests on weekends. I spent some of my time in the lake swimming. I had yet to pass Swimming 101 and was determined to do so as soon as possible. We also had training on water operations. The two months at Camp Buckner concluded with a patrolling exercise. At the end of the exercise were water obstacles, crossing wet logs thirty feet over the water, and sliding down a cable – dubbed the slide for life – and dropping into the water.

In late August we were back on the Academy grounds. This time my company was assigned the sixth floor of the brand new Eisenhower Hall. This building had been in progress for several years, with stone masons brought over from Italy to do the stone work. Everything had to blend into the dull gray atmosphere, and it seemed that stone masonry was a dying trade in the States. At West Point even the new had to look old. Moving meant relocating from the former barracks, where most of our belongings were in the storage rooms in the basement, to the top floor of Eisenhower Hall. It meant competing for the few carts we could use to haul our belongings. Living in barracks, overlooking the parade field known as the Plain, required that everything that could catch the public eye be kept perfect. Window shades had to be aligned and no items in the windows were to be seen by the gazing public.

This was the sophomore, or yearling, year. At West Point the sophomores are called yearlings and juniors are cows. I have no clue as to the origin of those names. After all, things are not necessarily logical at the Academy. Yearling year offered a new freedom of movement, and there were the new plebes. Most of the guys who had vowed to lay off plebes seemed to go out of their way to eat them up. As for me and my time, I had better things to do, like rock squad. In addition to the academic, athletic, and other requirements, there was also remedial swimming waiting for me. So the little children continued to act like mermaids in the pool while I attempted to tread water, bob and travel, and do my laps. I yearned for the day I would finally overcome my embarrassing, energy-zapping, and time-consuming plight.

The day came when Lt. Parker, who was as tired of seeing me as I was of seeing him, challenged me to take the swimming test. In accepting the challenge, I told myself that I would either pass the test or drown, because instructors stay dry. The last event was the 25 -meter underwater swim. My body told me after about halfway to the finish that it needed air, and I had to make by body follow my mind, which said, "I ain't coming up till I touch the opposite wall." Yes, the body is subservient to the mind. That was the last day I remember seeing Lt. Parker, except for an occasional flashback to the rock squad experience. I was then paroled from swimming until the validation test at graduation time.

Yearlings also had calculus. I had learned from the previous year how to prepare academically. By the second year we were regrouped according to ability, and the instructors teaching the classes of the less academically gifted tended to go more slowly and spend more time teaching. The entire second year was filled with required subjects heavy in the sciences. The key to science is knowing the formulas and how to use them. Once I became comfortable with the academic load, and free of the burden of remedial swimming, I was able to compete in intercollegiate track. I started with indoor and then outdoor track. Again I had more potential than talent. But competition is healthy, making us set goals and strive to achieve them. And if we don't do so well in competition, we have at least learned discipline in the process.

Social events now moved from the plebe hangout in Cullum Hall to the gymnasium. We were still restricted to the Academy grounds. The gym was cleaned on Saturdays and turned into a dance hall on Saturday nights. Girls were bused in from the local colleges. So the normal procedure was to scout out the array of young ladies lining the walls, grab a dance or two, and retreat back to the confines of one's room. And if you met someone really interesting you could chat over cookies and punch until the girls were whisked away on the buses at the end of the night. We could also attend a movie on Saturdays in the former riding stable, which was turned into the main academic building and named Thayer Hall.

This was the first year we could have radios and stereos in our rooms. Televisions were taboo all four years. During Christmas leave I ventured out to Chicago and Detroit before heading to Philly. The common factor between the two cities is COLD. You do not go strutting in thin clothing around the Great Lakes. After a short visit to Philadelphia, I headed back to the Academy early for a track meet in Syracuse, New York, another bone-chilling place. Things were back in full swing with the arrival of the corps and another academic semester. The bleak winter edged into spring and then the surfacing of national turmoil for the balance of 1968. The assassinations of Dr. Martin Luther King, Jr., and Robert Kennedy would reshape the conscience of America

The summer of 1968 arrived with the usual parades and pageantry. Graduation elevated my class to that of junior, or cow, status. It is at this point that cadets are allowed to go out into the real Army and serve in apprentice leadership positions. My assignment was Fort Polk, Louisiana. My buddy Willie Price, the Chicago connection, talked me into this one. Because we were low in academic standing our choices were limited. The smart boys got the good places, like Europe, Hawaii, Colorado, and California. I had leave first, then jetted out of Philadelphia to New Orleans. The big jet landed in the festival city and then I did the next leg to Lake Charles on Trans Texan Airline, a tree jumper local carrier. We were picked up and headed for Fort Polk whose closest town with a name was Leesville, nick named "Diseaseville," because men frequenting certain places often contracted sexually transmitted diseases. Not only was I going into bayou country, but this was my first trip to the Deep South. Louisiana is the Sportsman's Paradise. The first sport was trying to stay cool in the humid Louisiana summer. We were housed in the top floor of an old World War II wooden barracks which was divided into separate rooms. A fan and an occasional breeze were all the comfort provided. As it happened, we spent little time in there anyway.

My job was as assistant training officer in an infantry advanced individual training (AIT) company. Fort Polk was an Army Training Center with the mission of training new soldiers for Vietnam. Its Tiger Hill was a model Vietnamese village, complete with the realism of the war. The soldiers were ordinary people from the towns, cities, and farms of America. This was a reality check for me. The meager existence on a wooden Army post carved out of a swamp in western Louisiana contrasted sharply with the artificial world behind the granite walls of West Point.

My buddy Willie Price and I linked up with a young lieutenant stationed at Fort Polk and got treated to a grand tour of the surroundings. The much talked about Leesville still sported wooden sidewalks, hitching posts, and run-down buildings. We went to a party somewhere down what seemed like the longest and darkest road in Louisiana. Once the car's headlights were turned off the night was pitch black. Our maiden venture to the outskirts of post was enough exploration for me. I did get a chance to see some of Texas for the first time. Another lieutenant was going to Houston and invited me to ride with him and his wife. I saw miles of wide open, flat country.

Army life quickly develops into a series of routines. For the trainees and cadre it was up before light, physical training, and a full day's activities driven by the unit training schedule. This was infantry advanced individual training, and those soldiers' next stop would likely be Vietnam. Their training was rigorous and intensive in jungle tactics. My four-week adventure at Fort Polk was a struggle against relentless heat and humidity. It was evident that this environment was well suited to simulate Vietnam. This training ended in late August and we left for the return trip to cow year at the academy. We loaded the Army buses and headed for the airport at Lake Charles and the long trip back to the East Coast.

Being a junior, a cow, brought with it direct supervision over the plebe population. The cows were squad leaders and had to ride herd over the plebiscite. This meant inspections of their persons, rooms, and equipment; ensuring they performed their duties; disciplining them; and monitoring their academic progress. It also meant that you held significant power over them and could be a major influence in their lives. Some cows would use their status to wreak havoc on the plebes to make their lives challenging, or in other words, miserable. Cow year had the reputation of being the most difficult academic year, with electrical engineering, dubbed "juice," and hydraulic engineering, dubbed "fluids," being tough courses. I was not about to take any chances with an academic bust and set out with a good attitude to knock out the year.

The grading policy was such that you were always being tested, and one who was diligent during the beginning of the semester and achieved good grades could survive even with mediocre performances toward the end. The term was "coasting." This concept did not have much application in the real college world where students had to perform well on one or two big exams. I managed to maintain my grades without any undo hardship, and even participated in intercollegiate track and other activities.

Then finally it was senior year. The Class of 1970 had arrived at the top of the heap. The senior class has full responsibility for all the underlings. My senior summer was spent as a platoon leader for the second year cadets at Camp Buckner. This was a high energy job, which kept me moving from wake up call to lights out. The typical day consisted of physical training, breakfast, training, lunch, training, dinner, training, maintenance, and lights out. This was the summer of 1969, and because things were hot in Vietnam, the training emphasized small unit tactics and jungle warfare. This assignment gave me some good leadership experience and validated my decision to accept a commission in the infantry, which in all likelihood would be all that was left by the time they got to my name. The summers were the only time we saw our instructors in army fatigues and getting dirty. Imagine that, the ivory tower teachers were also real soldiers.

One of the weekends I was allowed off the post I found myself stranded in New York City after the last bus had left the Port Authority terminal for Highland Falls, the stop for West

Point. I found my way to Highway 9W and used my hitchhiking skills to get a ride. A group of guys picked me up in their beat-up van, where I found a place to hang onto in the back. The van smelled like a garbage truck, but at least I was not walking. This proved to be the most memorable ride I have ever had. Highway 9W is a winding two-, sometimes three-lane highway overlooking the Hudson River, with steep vertical embankments. The driver decided to race another vehicle around the mountain without regard for the double solid line or oncoming traffic. I prayed and hung on the entire time. The guys finally got me close to my destination, remarkably in one piece. I exited the vehicle weak-kneed and thankful to be alive. I gladly accepted my punishment of being restricted to quarters for returning late. That experience put an end to my hitchhiking days.

During the spring of 1970 our class was ushered into the auditorium in Thayer Hall for branch selection, which was according to class rank. As usual, the quotas for the Corps of Engineers, the executive agent for the building of America, were exhausted first, and those of us at the bottom of the class harbored no expectations for any branch other than infantry. However, the last few guys were shocked by their involuntary assignment to the air defense branch rather than the infantry. I chose the infantry, with my first assignment in Germany. I would train at Fort Benning, Georgia, before going overseas.

Two events occurred shortly before graduation. First the new cars my classmates ordered – Corvettes, Camaros, Firebirds, Mustangs, Chargers, Challengers – began to arrive. We could not have cars until the last semester. Although I had my brother's 1960 Mercury sequestered in Highland Falls, I got caught up in new car fever and purchased a 1970 Dodge Challenger instead of a used car. Then I met a feisty young lady who stole my heart. She was Jannie Wells, or Jean for short, a transplanted Alabamian.

Graduation was on June 3, 1970. It was a beautiful day at Michie Stadium, the football field, where graduation for the Class of 1970 was held. The graduating class included one more black cadet, Gary Steele, a star football player, and raised the number of new lieutenants of color to eight. Gary was originally in the Class of 1969, but had to repeat a year. With the infamous hat toss at the end of graduation, we were paroled from the confinement of the United States Military Academy into the general population of the United States Army.

Shortly thereafter I loaded my bride and all our worldly possessions into my metallic blue 1970 Dodge Challenger and headed south. I stopped in Virginia to visit my grandparents, to introduce Jean to them, and received the counsel of Grandpa Jack. He said, "Watch out for those Georgia crackers. They got some mean crackers down there." I thought to myself that they couldn't be any worse than the crackers in neighboring Prince Edward County who shut down the schools for five years rather than integrate them. Then after arriving in Columbus, Georgia, and in search of temporary housing I began to realize the wisdom of Grandpa Jack's counsel. While conducting a search for temporary housing I realized that equal housing had yet to be fully embraced in Columbus, Georgia, as rental agencies kept steering us to Pine Terrace. Pine Terrace was a housing project. As a result we purchased a mobile home and set it in a new mobile home park close to Fort Benning. We then went to Jean's home in the little town of Reform in western Alabama and picked up her son Thomas Christopher (Chris), and settled in as a new Army family.

CHAPTER FOUR

TRANSFORMATION

The assassination of Dr. Martin Luther King, Jr., in Memphis, Tennessee, on April 4, 1968, was a day of awakening for the entire nation. Riots broke out in over 100 cities, including Detroit and Washington, D.C., as soldiers from the 82nd Airborne Division were dispatched to guard the nation's capital. Dr. King's assassination would transform the conscience of America. I was a yearling then. My transformational day was April 5, 1968.

The New York Times had been delivered to the door by the plebes. Pictures of soldiers of the 82nd Airborne Division with their machine guns on the steps of the United States Capitol building covered the front page. Articles about the assassination of Dr Martin Luther, Jr., were vastly outnumbered by articles about the riots that had broken out all over the country. The talk of the mess hall was about the riots and condemnation of civil disobedience. While I was trying to eat my scrambled eggs with ham bits an angry white upperclassman turned to me and asked, "What do you people want?" I deflected the question back to him by suggesting that he ask the people he was referring to. The question, however, was valid and thought provoking for me because I had no firsthand experience with the frustration felt by those driven to the point of rioting and was just as dumbfounded as the white cadet. I too needed to know what my people wanted. I too wondered about the issues triggering black frustration and felt impotent to answer. I knew that the presence of black cadets at the Academy was the result of the civil rights movement. No service academy had a good track record regarding minority enrollment. There was only a handful of black cadets at West Point when Dr. King was assassinated. The world asked why this was happening. My fellow cadets were outraged and the comments from the law-and-order types included, "They ought to shoot them down in the streets." Questions posed to me included, "Why are your people doing this?" My response was, "I don't know." But I too needed to know why. Because I was from a background similar to that of the rioters and was ignorant concerning what was happening, it was not surprising that the future leaders of America's Army were even more ignorant. Most of these youngsters represented the best of America, and many came from generations of military men. The military is a closed society which has little contact with real-life issues such as poverty, homelessness, and unemployment. Military families are usually sequestered on tidy military posts with amenities like clubs, schools, gymnasiums, chapels, hospitals, post exchanges, and commissaries. They think that it is real life, but it is not. In the military you give orders and things happen. These pampered young men were in a cultural vacuum and were going to lead people from all walks of life. With the war in Vietnam going strong, young black men were being drafted into the Army primarily from the urban centers. I saw a great conflict on the horizon as the redneck southern-bred second lieutenants and the black city boy dropouts were going to serve together. Thus, I needed to know why.

I assumed that every black family in America had closely followed the civil rights movement since World War II. Politicians were once able to control people by limiting the information available to them. But World War II began to expose people to more information about the world around them. And racial inequality in America took a serious beating after the war as minorities and women refused to give up the opportunities they had first experienced when the country needed them for the war effort. I reflected on Rosa Parks and the Montgomery, Alabama, bus boycott, and the inspiring oratory and leadership of the young preacher Martin Luther King, Jr.

I reflected back to the bitter violence in Selma, Alabama, and elsewhere, perpetrated by whites trying to hold on to the old ways. My mind reflected back five years to August 25, 1963, and the March on Washington, which I watched intensely at home on the fussy black and white television. I also remembered the many journeys to segregated Virginia, with each trip choreographed with planned stops only at the service stations that would serve black people. Emergencies had to be dealt with along the side of the road.

I knew black folks cried over the death of John Kennedy and were heartbroken by the assassination of Martin Luther King, Jr. But I needed to know more about the history and rich legacy of African Americans to address the question of why my people were frustrated to the point of rioting. I trekked to the Cadet Library, a four-story monstrosity, to do some research.

I was astonished to find that there was a wealth of books by black writers. I was overwhelmed by the diversity of authors: Du Bois, Garvey, Baldwin, Ellison, King, and Cleaver. I got so excited over the opportunity to educate myself that I had to schedule my private reading, which was like dessert, after the main course, which was the academic requirements and other required cadet activities. My self-education became my passion.

To make time for my freelance reading I had to develop a more efficient way to accomplish my academic agenda. The first rule was that academics were a must and everything else had a lower priority. Once I got started with works by James Baldwin, Martin Luther King, John Hope Franklin, W.E.B. Du Bois, Malcolm X, and an assortment of other writers I was hooked. There were days when I would check out a handful of books from the library, read them, and return for more. The speed reading course really paid off.

The routine actually made me more efficient with my class work. I would complete my lessons as a prerequisite to reading for my personal enlightenment. Thereafter I felt adequately prepared for the white boys' inquiries about the behavior of black people. I felt a responsibility to be available to help educate our new lieutenants in waiting about racial issues. It would take the Army a while to muster the courage to openly discuss race in America, even though the Army was the leading institution for integration and social change. I sensed the calling to devote my life to helping others.

CHAPTER FIVE

GROWN FOLKS ARMY

Army officers are commissioned from several sources, including the Reserve Officer Training Corp (ROTC), Officer Candidate School (OCS), and direct commissions. Then each officer has to be trained in his specialty during an officer basic course conducted by his branch school. Because my branch was infantry I had to report to the Infantry School at Fort Benning, Georgia, nicknamed the Benning School for Boys, to attend the Infantry Officers Basic Course, and specialty training including airborne and ranger schools. West Pointers going into the other combat arms branches – armor, artillery, engineers, and signal – were first ushered through Fort Benning for airborne and ranger school before going to their basic branch schools at Forts Knox, Sill, Belvoir, and Gordon. The order of training for infantry lieutenants was airborne, infantry, and ranger school. Because we would be winter rangers, we would face harsh conditions in the mountains of Georgia and the swamps of Florida. The risk of cold weather injury made the challenge more daunting. I have never been so tired, cold, or hungry than in Ranger School. We received one meal, consisting of C-ration (combat ration of canned food), per day and harbored constant dreams of food, a bed, and being with our families. Sometimes we would sleepwalk and talk to trees. Unfortunately we lost one lieutenant during an airborne drop into Florida owing to high winds in the drop zone. The man was a seasoned skydiver. Frostbite was the most common and serious injury for winter rangers.

At the conclusion of my Fort Benning adventures I was off to Germany and the 3rd Armored Division. My initial assignment was with the 1st Battalion, 48th Infantry Regiment,

2nd Brigade, 3rd Armored Division in Gelnhausen, Germany. The 2nd Brigade housed at the Gelnhausen Kascerne, included two infantry battalions, an armor battalion, and an artillery battalion. My Battalion Commander was LTC John Swaren, Jr., a firm and fair leader who strived to enforce high standards. At my initial meeting he spelled out his expectations of his officers. Vietnam had devastated the junior officer corps. He handed me a magazine article showing an Army officer smoking marijuana with his men in Vietnam to better bond with them. He explained that such conduct was unacceptable. I was assigned to Bravo (B) Company, where I was given the Weapons Platoon, consisting of a mortar section with 81 mm mortars and an antitank section sporting the 106 mm Recoilless Rifle, which was later replaced with the TOW (Tubular Operated Wireless) missile. My company commander was a sloppy, overweight, laid-back West Pointer who provided little mentorship. He was on his way to Vietnam. The Company Executive Officer was an abrasive, overzealous, cussing Texas Aggie who made up for the CO's lack of assertiveness. He later became Company Commander. I gleaned leadership traits from two seasoned soldiers who were company commanders. They were Captain Charles Clark of Headquarters Company and Captain Arthur Holmes, Jr., of Charlie Company. Both were Vietnam veterans and former NCOs and graduates of Officer Candidate School (OCS). They were mature and displayed superior people and soldier skills.

My platoon lacked a Platoon Sergeant (E7) and was vastly under strength. A lack of maturity among my noncommissioned officers created a leadership void. They were Vietnam veterans who had survived there by exercising infantry riflemen's skills, and had not worked in their military occupational specialties (MOS) of indirect fire and antitank. They were promoted to Staff Sergeant (E6) based on meeting the promotion criteria of time in service and time in grade, but lacked the education and professional development of the NCOs of earlier times. As a new butter bar (second lieutenant) I was expecting my NCOs to be instrumental in training both me and the new soldiers. Such was not the case. Finally my battalion commander counseled me, informing me that I possessed more technical knowledge and leadership skills than my NCOs and that I had better get with the program and get my NCOs up to par.

My situation was not unique. Vietnam was consuming the Army's personnel and resources. America's Army in Germany was in desperate need of functional equipment, spare parts, maintenance assets, and training resources. Life usually revolved around the repetitive routine of unit maintenance: going to the motor pool and opening up our armored personnel carriers and cleaning stuff. The soldiers were spending too much time in garrison and too little time in the field. They had time on their hands for mischief. In addition the Army's problems of racial tension and drug abuse were magnified in Germany, with its mixed population of Vietnam veterans, called "short timers," awaiting their discharge from the Army and new soldiers, enlistees and draftees, arriving from their initial military training posts. There was an explosive mix of urban African American, Puerto Rican, "New York Ricans" (New York born soldiers of Puerto Rican descent), Mexican Latinos, and rural Caucasians vying for attention. Many of our Latino soldiers struggled with English and were studying English as a second language. Despite that, our Mexican-American First Sergeant refused to communicate in Spanish. "Don't speak that shit around me," he would admonish the Latinos who attempted to communicate in Spanish.

I began to use some of my promising, newly-arrived soldiers, fresh out of advanced infantry training, to train the platoon. We would study the Army Field Manuals and review them with the NCOs to school them in doctrine, and then practice our craft. I soon learned that some of my NCOs lacked reading and comprehension skills. The lessons learned were that rank, status, and position did not equate to competence and that military rank was immaterial in getting the job done. There were three major training areas in Germany: Grafenfeld, Hoensfeld, and Wildflecken. The battalion usually conducted three training events each year, one at each major training area. Moving to the training areas was a mini-mobilization that included moving all vehicles and equipment by train and wheeled vehicle to the training area. Other training opportunities occurred during the winter months, when the frozen ground provided an opportunity to maneuver over the geography encompassing our assigned area of responsibility. These were the Cold War years, and we were staring down the Soviet Union and preparing for the next world war or nuclear holocaust. Our area of responsibility included the Fulda Gap, a likely high-speed avenue of approach for the Soviets into West Germany.

I received a rude awakening concerning leadership when I arrived at one of the training sites. Several of my soldiers were summoned to the battalion commander's office, where criminal charges were levied against them under the Uniform Code of Military Justice (UCMJ) for extortion and robbery. They were placed in pretrial confinement and whisked off to the Army Disciplinary Barracks in Mannheim. When I learned of the situation I raced to LTC Swaren's office to request that my soldiers be released to me and allowed to participate in training pending their courts martial. They were good soldiers, or so I thought, and productive members of the platoon. I also asked why I was not informed of this intended action and given a chance to discipline my soldiers. Colonel Swaren told me that as a result of his open-door policy he learned that my soldiers, along with several other black soldiers, were running an extortion ring in the barracks and he had to take action.

I later learned from one of the extortion victims, a quiet white draftee, that there was tension and chaos in the barracks, and a small band of black guys had demanded "protection money" to keep the lid on things. I asked him why he had not approached me before going higher. His perception was that because I was black I would do nothing. He lacked confidence that I would handle the problem. I learned from that experience that a leader must know and win the confidence of his subordinates. From then on I regularly held open sessions with my soldiers and stayed aware of what was going on. I received my convicted soldiers back after they served their sentences. Normally returning convicted soldiers are reassigned to other units. My soldiers requested to stay in my platoon. They were allowed to remain and served admirably until they met their service obligation. I later crossed paths with one of the rehabilitated soldiers, and we served together in the Army Reserve from which he retired as a Master Sergeant (E8).

My next assignment was as the Battalion S3 (Air) which in reality made me the Assistant Operations Officer, because there were few air assets to coordinate. I assisted the S3, a major, and was involved with training, plans, and operations. I enjoyed the job but left it when I was tapped as the Brigade Race Relation Officer, as the Army aggressively pursued solutions to its mounting racial tension. The Army as a leader in integration in America had institutional knowledge that changing behavior is essential to changing attitudes. Thus race relations training seminars became mandatory. The seminars first started with senior leaders: colonels, lieutenant colonels, and sergeant majors, and worked their way down to soldiers of every rank. The old soldiers at first resisted the concept, claiming that the only color they saw was army green. Again, a change of behavior usually precedes a change of attitude. Once the officers and NCOs attended the program after being ordered to do so, they began to support it. The race relations seminars were structured to encourage the free exchange of thoughts and beliefs among the attendees, with everyone having an equal voice regardless of rank. The strategy began to foster deeper understanding among the diverse group of people. The Department of Defense established the Defense Equal Opportunity Management Institute (DEOMI). The Army Equal Opportunity Program was then formalized to foster equality of opportunity without regard to color, race, religion, gender, or national origin, and it established monitoring criteria using statistical measurements.

Racial tension in Gelnhausen diminished but did not go away. One evening I was summoned to the artillery battalion, where some disgruntled black soldiers had taken over the battalion headquarters in protest of disciplinary action against a black soldier. The protesting soldiers claimed racism on the part of the chain of command, which they perceived as meting out harsher punishment to black soldiers than to white soldiers. A soldier had been formally charged with an offense and was headed to pretrial confinement when his buddies intervened. I was asked to talk to the soldiers. After several hours of listening to them I realized that the poisonous power of perception had corrupted their reasoning capability. In the end I was able to squelch the situation by conveying their frustration to their chain of command, and delivering to them the facts regarding their complaints, which were in direct contradiction of their perception. Once the communication process was completed and the soldiers were reminded that they too were in jeopardy of disciplinary action, they backed off and surrendered the occupied building.

Germany was a good experience for my family. We initially lived in the German community on the second floor of an elderly couple's home. Although hampered by the language barrier, we got along well and the couple adored Chris. Once after running out of hot water, I summoned the landlord who showed me that the kerosene-fired hot water heater for the kitchen and bathtub had to be lit for each use. Only the bathroom sink had on-demand hot water from the small heater attached to it. So much for American standards. I sensed that I would have to do a lot of cultural learning during my tour. After living in the local community for about six months we moved to the sixth floor (no elevator) in one of the government housing areas. Our housing area was shared by officers and NCOs, allowing us to intermingle with a lot of NCOs. We got plenty of exercise negotiating the six flights of stairs several times a day.

Europe was exciting and interesting. We took advantage of the opportunity to travel, and visited many Western European countries, including West Germany, Austria, Switzerland, France, Italy and Spain. Our favorite destination was Spain's Costa Brava. When we traveled I had a little translation book, and used the book *Europe on Five Dollars a Day* to find accommodations. My standard operating procedure was to learn the greetings of each country and greet the merchants in their language no matter how horrible I sounded. We found ourselves being treated cordially after our best imitation of *Guten Abend, buenos dias,* or *ciao.* On one trip we crossed the Straits of Gibraltar by car ferry and visited Morocco and one of its bazaars. "Hey, brother, I watch your car." I turned to see a young boy maybe age 10 or 11 who saw us pull up in our VW Beetle with the required international sticker advertising "USA." " Brother, sister, I watch your car while you shop. O.K." How much, I asked. "Not much. I show you around." I thought it best to pay the ransom and have a car to return to. I gave the lad some money and he nodded to an older man perched in a corner of the lot. "What you want, sister?" He proceeded to escort us through the bazaar and give his secret nod to the merchants who rewarded him for bringing in customers. After we parted I saw him negotiate with others in a variety of languages. It was amazing to observe how he could move from one language to another.

After Germany my next assignment was Fort Dix, New Jersey, which I had requested to be closer to Philadelphia and my folks. Dad's medical condition had deteriorated due to acute diabetes and kidney failure, and Mom was just about worn out from taking care of him. His diminishing eyesight was a signal that he was approaching his final stage of life. Fort Dix was a training post under the control of the Army Training and Doctrine Command (TRADOC). Basic combat training was Fort Dix's main business. When I reported to the Training Brigade Commander, he inquired of my future plans. I told him I was planning to leave the Army upon the completion of my five year obligation, which was a year away. I was scheduled to be a company commander but was instead reassigned as the post Billeting Officer. I assume the brigade commander did not want to waste a coveted company command assignment on a defector. Billeting operations included managing both appropriated and nonappropriated fund activities. Nonappropriated funds activities operated as independent businesses and had to sustain themselves without the infusion of taxpayer dollars. As Billeting Officer I was responsible for temporary housing, including Bachelor Officer Quarters (BOQ), Visiting Officer Quarters (VOQ), the Doughboy Inn, and barracks for Reservists on annual training.

Reserve soldiers performing their annual training, usually two weeks in the summer and fall, inhabited Fort Dix in great numbers, with Army Reserve Training Divisions assisting in the training of new recruits. The billeting branch provided the temporary officer housing set up for the reservists. Until then I was unfamiliar with the Army's Reserve Component, Army Reserve, and Army National Guard. After all, I was a Regular Army Officer (RA), with guaranteed career longevity, who had little association with the traditional reservists. The only Reserve Officers I knew were those on initial active duty completing their ROTC (Reserve Officer Training Corps) obligations. For the uninformed, reservists were a bunch of imitation soldiers, dubbed "weekend warriors." Billeting operations kept me in frequent contact with reservists who came in two categories, Troop Program Unit (TPU) and Individual Ready Reserve (IRR). I am glad I came to know the reserve component side of the Army. I opted to take advantage of a master's degree program at neighboring McGuire Air Force Base. Central Michigan University (CMU) offered distance learning programs at satellite campuses on some Air Force bases. CMU ran weekend programs requiring Friday evening, Saturday, and Sunday attendance on alternating weekends. We took one course at a time and could complete one course a month after 40 hours of class attendance. If the class offerings lined up right, the master's program could be completed in a year. I opted for Business Management. The pace was intense, and demanding. We had a mixed group of active duty service members, retirees, and civilians. I found that dealing with one class in a compressed fashion was the ideal learning process, because there was only one course to deal with at a time.

Army officers are assigned additional duties and placed on personnel boards at the discretion of their commander. Both in Germany and at Fort Dix, I was occasionally placed on administrative boards convened to separate nonperforming soldiers from the Army. These unproductive, problem soldiers included convicted felons, deserters, AWOLs (absent without leave), and soldiers in civilian confinement. They were mostly young black and Latino soldiers who had become disciplinary problems or received civilian convictions. The Army needed to remove them from its rolls and was required by Army Regulations to conduct separation boards composed of a group of disinterested officers and NCOs. Each soldier, or respondent, was entitled to a representative. The government's case was presented by a recorder, the equivalent of a prosecutor. The respondent was represented by an officer appointed to represent him. The separation boards were mostly held ex parte because the soldiers were locked up or had disappeared from the Army. At Fort Dix I began working with Army JAG officers which triggered my interest in the law.

I discovered that some of the JAG types had previously served in other branches of the Army before attending law school. I was told that those of average intelligence with strong determination could complete law school. In addition I discovered that some of my West Point classmates whose intelligence level mirrored mine were in law school. So I began exploring the possibility of a legal career. With my meager undergraduate grades I had an added incentive to obtain the master's degree from CMU. I purchased a study guide to prepare for the Law School Aptitude Test (LSAT). After applying to several schools I requested an interview based on the advice of a classmate who informed me that law schools usually maintained a waiting list of qualified applicants who were not offered admission. In the event of unfilled seats, schools go down the waiting list to fill last-minute vacancies. I managed to get an interview with Rutgers University Law School at Camden, New Jersey. I was on a court martial panel earlier that day for a soldier charged with burglary. It was my first experience with the criminal justice process. It only took a short time to convict the soldier, and I was off to Camden for my interview before a committee of students and faculty.

Dad died on August 2, 1975, while I was in the process of leaving active duty. He had earlier suggested that I stay in the Army, which I found strange because he never spoke about the Army, nor had he shared his World War II experience with us. I sensed that he saw a new Army far different from the segregated Army he served in during World War II. Also, his brother Jack, who was a career soldier, led a pretty comfortable life. I had made up my mind to divorce the Army. I had secured two manufacturing job offers, one with Johnson & Johnson Products, New Brunswick, New Jersey, and the other with Philip Morris USA, Richmond, Virginia. The moving company was at my quarters loading our household furniture when

I received a phone call from Rutgers Law School informing me that I could enter school the following week if I had my tuition money. I had some savings because, in anticipation of going to law school, I was earning additional money delivering the morning newspaper, the *Philadelphia Inquirer,* on post. The papers arrived around 4:30 a.m., and relying on my childhood experience, I usually had the daily papers delivered by 5:30 a.m. and the bulky Sunday papers by 6:30 a.m. I had also saved my unused military leave to cash in when I left the Army. In addition, I was eligible for educational benefits, a monthly stipend from the GI Bill administered by the Veterans Administration. This was a great opportunity, except for one thing. Finding an affordable place to live in New Jersey proved to be an insurmountable task. Because there was nothing available on such short notice I had to abandon the chance of attending to law school that year.

My next option was the job with Johnson & Johnson in north Jersey, which would allow me to stay in the area and reapply to Rutgers the following year. Again, affordable housing was the obstacle. There was no affordable housing in North Jersey either. I then executed my final option, which was the job at Philip Morris in Richmond, Virginia. Richmond was somewhat familiar territory because I had many relatives there and had passed through numerous times en route to my grandparents' place in Burkeville. I resigned my Regular Army Commission and left active duty on September 11, 1975. While out-processing from the Army, I was asked if I wanted a reserve commission. I said yes and was sworn into the United States Army Reserve. Thus I had broken a nine-year umbilical cord of Army nurturing and development. I had divorced the Army, or so I thought, and was on my own.

I have recently come to realize the impact of the military bonding process, wherein service members usually consummate a union with the military before getting married. It is an unusual but important relationship. Senior military leaders will never admit it, but they prefer that a new soldier be grounded in a strong union with the military before taking on a spouse. Look at the recruiting and training processes, which target young, healthy people, who are thoroughly screened for suitability and then separated from society and meticulously molded into a new product. They must assume the identity and values of their new family as their bodies and minds are transformed into those of soldiers, sailors, marines, and airmen. The Army will infuse massive doses of Army Values – Loyalty, Duty, Respect, Selfless Service, Honor, Integrity, and Personal Courage – into her Soldiers. And Soldiers swear by the Soldiers' Creed and promise always to place the mission first. U.S. Soldiers believe that they can do any and all things. They must do what they are ordered to do because they protect our country and the American way of life.

High School Photo, 1966

Lt. Robinson, Germany 1972

Brig. General Leo A. Brooks presents Capt. Bruce Robinson the distinguished graduate award and diploma for Discussion Leaders' Course, September 29, 1978.

Bruce Robinson

G1

West Point, Class of 1970

Brigadier General Promotion, December 2000

Baghdad, Iraq, April 2005:
CSM William Grocott, MG Bruce
Robinson,BG Richard Sherlock

MG Bruce Robinson with "mentors" MG Charles Wilson, DCG,
USAR Command and MG Robert Smith, CG 84th Division,
change of command dinner, August 1, 2002

The Soldier must pledge his loyalty/love to the nation above all else. Soldiers are made to bond together and react as a team in life-and-death situations. They usually join the military when they are single, and their military status brands them as the best of society. They are clean-cut, healthy, drug-free individuals with good paying jobs with guaranteed benefits. They are desirable to others and are prone to attract interested partners. Then once a soldier marries, his spouse becomes the mistress and the military remains the marital partner. Efforts are made to indoctrinate the spouse to military life and gain her buy-in. There is little tolerance for a rebellious mate challenging the preexisting union with the military. It would be considered disloyal to suggest that one's spouse should garner as much affection or attention as the Army, Navy, Marine Corps, Air Force, or Coast Guard. Then wartime experiences increase the military bond and places stress on marriages as the band of brothers and sisters hang tough together for their mutual survival. That is what sustains the warrior. That is what sustains our military. Consider it one of the occupational hazards of serving the nation.

Let's use Army officers as an example. One of the admissions criteria for the service academies is that a person must never have been married nor have a support obligation. Then after joining the Army as a West Point or ROTC Cadet, there is usually four years of grooming for the eventual prearranged union with the Army. The goal is for the cadets to bond with the Army and stick around forever as officers. Upon graduation the new lieutenants swear their allegiance to the Nation and the Army above all else. Should one marry, the spouse will be reminded of the pre-existing marital contract, and attempts will be made to indoctrinate the new wife or husband on the need to yield the relationship to the military for the sake of the soldier, the Army, and the nation. The bride will be bribed to remain silent as her soldier pursues his first love with enticements of promotions, pay raises, nicer housing, education, and better assignments. Spouses will also bond together in support groups for the common good. In the event they grow weary of the Army's seduction of their mate, they learn that it is usually easier to separate from their soldier than it is for the soldier to separate from the Army, because there is a pre-arranged union with the Army, a contractual obligation.

PART III: REAL WORLD REALITY

CHAPTER SIX

JURISPRUDENCE

In 1975 Philip Morris was one of Richmond's largest civilian employers. Some families contained multiple generations of Philip Morris workers. Richmond and her surrounding counties' young people who lacked ambition viewed a job with Philip Morris as utopia because it paid well and had good benefits.

I accepted the job of production supervisor at Philip Morris. After the required company training I was assigned to a production line in the new cigarette plant on the night shift. Philip Morris was going through the consolidation of several old plants into a modern, automated facility. There were a variety of jobs ranging from the hot and dirty stemmery plant, where raw tobacco was removed from storage barrels called hogsheads and processed, to machine operation in the climate-controlled new plant with high-speed cigarette-making machines cranking out millions of cigarettes per day during three work shifts. Philip Morris was a caste society, where the older, unionized workers reigned by seniority. Job positions, work shifts, and even vacations were according to seniority. The hottest vacation week for local hunters was the opening of deer-hunting season in early November.

The highest paid workers were the "fixers," or machine maintenance crew consisting of mechanics, mill workers, and electricians who kept the machines humming. They usually waited in the break room overlooking the production floor until needed. Strict union rules set rigid separation of job standards. It was an inefficient system whereby, when a mechanic needed to fix a machine part inside a cabinet, he had to summon help to open the machine's cabinet and get to the part. Only the mill worker could open the cabinet. The electrician would disconnect the power, and the mechanic could then fix the part. Next in the pecking order of job superiority was the cigarette-making machine operator, followed by the packing machine operator. However, loyal workers with leadership potential could be elevated to nonunion supervisory positions.

The production floor organizational scheme resembled that of the Army. The line supervisor had a row of machines cranking out a specific brand of cigarette, and was the equivalent of a lieutenant platoon leader. The bay supervisor was in charge of a department consisting of several operating lines and was the equivalent of a captain company commander. The group or shift supervisor was like a battalion commander, overseeing all production in the various bays during a given shift. The morning shift operated from 7:00 a.m. to 3:00 p.m., the afternoon shift from 3:00 to 11:00 p.m., and the night shift from 11:00 p.m. to 7:00 a.m. The new high-speed machines were still being tweaked for faster and faster production and the shifts were in competition to outdo each other and to set production records. Quality was an important consideration, and there was constant monitoring of the tobacco content, the rolled cigarette appearance, and the packaging. The slightest imperfection could result in an angry supervisor ordering finished products pulled off conveyors and torn up to retrieve the tobacco for reuse.Industry, unlike the military, did not practice equal opportunity, and operated on the good old boy fraternization system with impunity. For example if a supervisor had a romantic relationship with a subordinate, the subordinate was likely to get maintenance problems resolved quickly. The attitude was that those who disliked such practices could move on to other employment.

Philip Morris expected to lose most of the new line supervisors, who usually were a mix of hourly workers elevated to management, recent college graduates, and retired or separating military personnel. As predicted, most former young officers departed for new employment and the retired NCOs hung on. I soon recognized that I would not be staying with Philip Morris any longer than was absolutely necessary. First, I did not believe in the product. I had hated tobacco since I was a kid pulling tobacco on Grandpa Jack's farm. Cigarette tobacco is laced with aromatic flavoring such as wine and licorice, designed to hook people. To me it was an addictive and toxic product. BUT it was blasphemy to think evil of a product intentionally designed to make smokers addicts. After all, tobacco was profitable, and Virginia's largest cash crop. Tobacco had fed and clothed many generations of Virginians and when the U.S. market began to falter after the required warning label: "THIS PRODUCT MAY BE HAZARDOUS TO YOUR HEALTH," tobacco manufacturers tapped into the emerging foreign markets in Asia and Africa to export the great American addiction. In any event, an employee owes his employer enthusiasm and loyalty in exchange for a paycheck. I knew that I would have to move on. Of the six former Army officers who were hired together, all left within a year except one.

I commuted from Richmond to McGuire Air Force Base in New Jersey to complete my last class for the master's degree with CMU. I again applied to several law schools when I arrived in Richmond, including Rutgers, Howard, and the University of Richmond. We purchased a small starter home and settled in South Richmond in an older 1950ish style subdivision of modest homes. I secured a VA loan and was now close to living the American Dream of home ownership and job security. The small Cape Cod house wasn't a castle but an affordable home in an area of Richmond that had been annexed from neighboring Chesterfield County. It was adjacent to U.S. Highway 360, which my family had traveled many times on our way to Nottoway County. The subdivision's policy limiting ownership to Caucasians was no longer enforceable, thanks to a ruling of the United States Supreme Court invalidating restrictive covenants based on race. I settled into the routine of the night shift at Philip Morris, working from 11:00 p.m. to 7:00 a.m. – and hated it. I am not a night person, and had trouble trying to force my body to change its natural rhythm for five days, and then requiring it to function as designed from 7:00 a.m. Friday until 9:30 p.m. Sunday, which constituted my weekend.

That routine was interrupted in the late spring of 1976, when I received an acceptance letter from the T.C. Williams School of Law, University of Richmond. I consulted with Jean, and we figured out a way to make it work. I accepted the offer, despite having few savings and little time to prepare to enter school in mid-August. Fortunately I had obtained my first ever credit card from the Bank of Virginia, and paid the first semester tuition with it. My monthly VA check would pay the mortgage and some utilities, but because I needed more money I considered joining the Army Reserve. I recalled seeing signs to an Army Reserve unit in South Richmond near Philp Morris. I did an unscientific search for a reserve unit by opening the telephone book and looking up "U.S. Government," then "U.S. Army," and stopped at the first Army Reserve unit listed, which was Headquarters, 80th Division. One telephone call and a subsequent interview netted me an assignment as the Assistant Equal Opportunity Officer. I intended to serve in the Army Reserve for three years, but I ended up serving for 32 years.

It is true that the most difficult part of law school is getting accepted. I don't know how I got accepted to the University of Richmond but I am thankful that I did. I suspect the T.C. Williams School of Law was behind the integration curve, because its first black graduate, a retired Army colonel, had only graduated a few years prior to my entry in 1976. The entering class was a cross-section of America, with a blend of recent undergraduates, former military officers, teachers, preachers, and retirees reshaping their careers. The admissions officer seemed to know everyone by name. I assume my master's degree from CMU garnered me consideration because my West Point grades and LSAT scores were unimpressive.

Initially I felt intimidated by my younger, smart classmates, who were fresh out of college. Our orientation included study tips and pointers on how to manage the workload. Once we settled into the mandatory subjects for first-year law school it became obvious to me that it was impossible to read all the case law that established the precedents for our Common Law. I viewed law school as an academic institution of repetitive legalese, given the Socratic form of instruction. To me law school offered little in the way of practical application, but at least provided the traditional rite of passage to becoming a lawyer. My daily routine consisted of attending classes in the morning and early afternoon. The late afternoon was for studying and cooking for the family. Jean was working part-time and completing her undergraduate degree. I passed all the major grocery stores en route to school, and using newspaper coupons and store specials, we managed to feed the family on an austere budget. There were a lot of tuna casseroles, spaghetti, and chili. But everyone was a student, and being a student requires sacrifice.

At the end of each week I reviewed my class notes and made a consolidated list of the principles of law for that week. I concentrated on understanding legal principles instead of the historical legalism behind them. My consolidated notes provided my study material in preparing for final exams. Sometimes I would participate in study groups but preferred to go it alone, especially when preparing for exams. We had access to our instructors' previous tests, which gave us an idea as to what to expect on the examinations. After passing my first semester classes with average grades, I sensed that law school was manageable. After completing the first year of school I decided to speed up the process by attending the summer sessions that offered a semester of study.

After hearing horror stories about the bar examination, and seeing the trepidation in the senior class, I began to pay closer attention to the subjects that would be tested in the bar examination. Even some of the brightest students failed the bar exam. I started early in my preparation, and set my goal to take the examination in July 1978 right before graduation that August. Nearly everyone took a separate bar review course designed to prepare graduates for the bar examination. I secured the job of setting up the classroom for each bar review session, which spared me the tuition fee. Bar review courses were straight-shooting, designed solely as preparation for the pending bar exam. They were not designed for academic enrichment.

Over the years the bar review institutes had deciphered the contents of the bar examinations, and offered tidbits of information on the substantive law and on techniques for passing the bar exam.

Virginia's bar examination was held twice a year, February in Richmond and July in Roanoke. It covered two days and had two parts, multistate and essay. The multistate portion covered universal law common throughout the country. It was a multiple-choice computer-scored test. The test contained a brief legal scenario, followed by questions at the end. Speed was imperative. During the review course we were conditioned to read fast, identify the issue, then select the best answer and move on. Only if time permitted were we to go back and rethink a question, because usually your first answer is the best one. I was thankful that I had four years of exposure to those types of tests at West Point. And I came to appreciate the value of the mind games of Beast Barracks, "Bugle Notes," and The Days, which forced me to memorize so many details.

The essay portion covered Virginia-specific law and required written answers. Here brevity counted and short, direct answers in legible handwriting were the key. I reduced my entire bar review study material to three-by-five cards which I studied constantly and memorized. I also made a cassette tape of the material and listened to it constantly on my battery-operated tape player – in the car, while exercising, cleaning – to saturate my brain with legal principles. Most other things were put on hold during my final preparation for the bar examination. My classmate Brenda Friend Briggs rode with me to Roanoke to take the bar exam. She was a graduate of Virginia State College (Virginia State University) and grew up in what was then segregated rural Chesterfield County. The route was U.S. Highway 360 West, then onto Highway 307, right past Grandma Mary's house, then U.S. Highway 460 West to Roanoke. I stopped to tell Grandma they we would return in two days for dinner. I made my reservation at a motel close to the Roanoke Civic Center, the test site, and spent the afternoon before the first day of tests reviewing my notes in final preparation for the multistate exam. Once it was it was over I did a brain dump and concentrated on my notes for the essay portion. After the bar exam we headed back toward Richmond. Grandma Mary had a delicious meal ready, complete with blackberry cobbler. I would never have imagined in my youth that this familiar highway would be my path to great opportunity.

We were told to expect the July results in October. We knew that when the results arrived a small envelope in your mailbox meant you had passed. A large envelope containing a new application was sent to those who failed the exam. I had met my goal of completing law school in two calendar years and taking the bar examination. I graduated in August 1978 and reported immediately to Fort Benning, Georgia, to complete my Advanced Infantry Officer Course. Law school was over and I pondered my options. Again my grades were average, but because I intended to enter into private legal practice, grades were of no consequence provided I pass the bar examination. I had eyed the old deteriorating section on lower Hull Street on Richmond's Southside as a possible office location. Hull Street is U.S. Highway 360, and slices Richmond east to west. We had traveled it many times going to and from Nottoway County. I casually looked for office space close to the Manchester Courthouse, which served South Richmond. Though the area was run down, some signs of revitalization were appearing. I suspected that rent would be cheap on the old business thoroughfare.

I went to my mailbox across from the house on the day bar results were to arrive. I slowly opened the mailbox as I prayed. I peered inside and pulled out a small envelope from the Virginia Bar Examiners. I had made the cut and was to be sworn in before the Virginia Supreme Court. My license reads "Bruce Edwin Robinson, Attorney and Counselor of Law." After the admission ceremony I was licensed to practice law in Virginia. I was now credentialed to practice law and represent clients – except that I lacked practical experience. I hoped to serve more as a counselor of law and prevent legal problems, but the attorney at law and trial work would win out.

CHAPTER SEVEN

BARRISTERVILLE

"Barrister" is a fancy title for lawyer. One of my buddies nicknamed me the Barrister. Some think he is saying "banister," and view me as someone to lean on.

In preparation for opening my office I sought out a seasoned attorney who would allow me to follow him around and shadow his moves. My mentor was Attorney Harrison Bruce. Like many of the middle-aged lawyers in Richmond, he was a veteran of World War II, and had taken advantage of the GI Bill to obtain his education. He was a sole practitioner with a substantial real estate practice. He allowed me to tag along with him and observe. He taught me how to conduct real estate title examinations and offered advice on how to handle criminal cases. I became familiar with trial work by sitting in the back of courtrooms observing the attorneys, defendants, judges, and court personnel. I intensified my search for office space on Hull Street in late 1978 and met a retired attorney who hung around his aging, unkempt office most of the day. He owned a lot of real estate in the area and was the neighborhood historian, landlord, and loan shark. He too was a World War II veteran, with a lot of time on his hands. We chatted for extended periods of time as he offered his take on the practice of law. He gave me the name of the owner of the vacant law office next door to him and suggested I call the owner, who was now a sitting a judge.

Judge Arlin Ruby sat in the Juvenile and Domestic Relations District Court (Juvenile Court) for the City of Richmond, and was the owner of the storefront building, which was configured into offices with partitions. Judge Ruby was also a World War II veteran and offered to sell me the building after pointing out the repairs it needed. He was uninterested in renting it, because if he maintained ownership I would be unable to appear before him owing to conflict of interest. With no money and no income, I thought purchasing real estate was out of the question. However, the judge referred me to his bank. I submitted a proposal to the bank, which agreed to finance the building provided they also get a second mortgage lien on my home, and that I maintain my business accounts there. I closed on the building and, after some sprucing up with a coat of paint and some cheap carpeting, was open for business in early January of 1979. The roof had some serious leaks, which required me to run to the office during heavy rains to dump the buckets I had positioned to collect the rain water. I hired a part-time secretary, a college student, with the understanding that we would learn together. I had my name painted on the plate glass window of the storefront building and was now a lawyer in search of clients. I was broke but was open for business. One of my buddies gave me his old VW Karmann Ghia that had been sitting in his backyard collecting bird droppings. Because it had a weak battery I had to park it on a hill, just in case I had to push it to jump start it.

I visited the courtrooms of the Manchester Courthouse, three blocks down the street from my office, and introduced myself to the judges. I then wrote a letter to the senior judge and asked to be placed on the court appointment list for indigent criminal defendants. My first paying client needed a will, which I prepared on a Royal electric typewriter on loan from my Aunt Elaine. I managed to get a few traffic cases and was placed on the court appointment list, because few lawyers were willing to face off with the Circuit Court judges on the Southside. Judge William Eldridge Spain was an icon, the historian of Old Manchester, which was at one time an independent city. It had merged with the City of Richmond, but the Virginia Constitution required that a courthouse be maintained south of the James River. There were two court venues in Richmond, with Southside having the reputation as the tougher one because of the Circuit Court Judges. Judge Spain tended to take a long time to decide a case and never missed an opportunity to reminisce about Old Manchester or historical trivia. Judge Frank A.S. Wright was like a bulldog and ran his courtroom like a battalion commander. He intimidated everyone, defendants, witnesses, lawyers, policemen, and probation officers alike.

Judge Wright accelerated my development. He gave me my start by putting me on the rotating court appointment list. After I tried a few cases before him he took an interest in my development. After a significant case he would summon me and the young Commonwealth Attorney (prosecutor) into his chambers and critique our performances. "Robinson, why did you do such and such?" He would then provide valuable advice on trial tactics. He laid out his simple philosophy. "Robinson, I don't want you embarrassing yourself or this state in some fancy New York or Philadelphia courtroom, so you better get it right." I was summoned to his office more than once to correct legal papers submitted to him. His secretary would call me. "Mr. Robinson, Judge Wright wants to see you in his chambers now." I would drop whatever

I was doing and race down to the courthouse. "Robinson, what is this? You expect me to sign this?" He instructed me on how to correct the documents and sent me back to my office to correct them. I was embarrassed by the clerical errors he would find, despite what I thought was thorough editing. I appreciated his mentorship and incorporated his advice into my law practice.

Over time I learned his method of operation. I gained an appreciation of his sentencing philosophy and attempted to prepare my clients for what they should expect as a sentence. At that time there were no sentencing guidelines, so a judge could sentence as he saw fit within the range of permissible punishment. For example, a grand larceny conviction carried from one to twenty years incarceration in the penitentiary; or up to twelve months in jail and/or a fine. A Presentence Report was a snapshot of a defendant's history and was used by judges to sentence convicted felons. Judge Wright was prone to hand down long sentences, with most of the time suspended for first time offenders. He was unsympathetic with repeat offenders. It was not uncommon for him to hand down a 20-year sentence for burglary when other judges were giving 10 years. Judge Wright expected realistic arguments at sentencing hearings and advised: "Robinson when you argue at sentencing give me a recommendation that I can say yes to." In other words, be realistic and don't argue for probation for someone caught breaking into his neighbor's home. At that time most felons were eligible for parole after serving a small portion of their sentence. Virginia now uses sentencing guidelines, in an attempt to standardize sentences throughout the state. Parole has also become more difficult, with felons now serving substantially their entire sentence.

In Virginia criminal juries determine the sentence, and a judge seldom if ever tampers with their recommendation. However, for most offenses a jury is not privy to a defendant's criminal background unless he testifies during the trial. Sometimes you have to risk a jury trial to mitigate a defendant's sentence. I recall one occasion when my client had an extensive criminal record and was caught by an eyewitness coming out of a burglarized residence. He was charged with burglary and grand larceny. He elected to take a jury trial rather than accept the 30 years offered by the Commonwealth Attorney. I cleaned him up for trial, had him sit upright, pay attention, and stay quiet during the trial. Using the Frank Wright philosophy of jury selection I kept all the older women (motherly types) on the jury panel and used my preemptory strikes to eliminate the middle-aged men who appeared to be leader types or critical thinkers like engineers and managers. During closing arguments the Commonwealth Attorney, who gets the first and last closing argument, argued to bury the guy with 20 or 30 years. Defense counsel only gets one chance to address the jury during closing arguments. The only thing I could realistically argue was that the defendant had been caught red-handed, and fortunately the property had been recovered. I asked the jury for a reasonable sentence based strictly on the evidence presented. The jury came back with a sentence of one year each for the burglary and grand larceny. Victory in the criminal arena is not an acquittal but the best deal for your client.

Exposure from court-appointed work fueled my criminal practice. This became the base of my legal practice, though I also handled some real estate, bankruptcy, personal injury, and family/domestic relations law. I soon eliminated domestic relations work, which is probably the most emotionally draining area of law, as feuding parties try to draw their attorneys' emotions into the fight. My most memorable client was a lady with serious psychological issues who elected to leave her husband. She was from a good family and was a well-educated middle-aged schoolteacher. Her purse resembled a drug store, filled as it was with antipsychotic medication. Her husband was a hardworking bricklayer with a limited education. He had built a nice home and provided well for his wife and their daughter. The lady had decided, however, to take off with a recently released felon, with whom she roamed the country. She once called me in hysterics from the Midwest, either Indiana or Illinois, where she had run out of money, and wanted an immediate increase in her temporary spousal support. I explained to her that she would have to appear at a hearing, and that support is based on need. Further, because she had left her employment and abandoned her family to shack up with a thug, she was unlikely to be allowed an increase in support payments. I advised her that she needed professional help and should return home immediately to her support system. Her calls came in regularly until she was finally penniless and forced to ditch her criminal boyfriend and return home.

My law practice eventually evolved into mostly bankruptcy, criminal, real estate, and personal injury work, with some uncontested divorces and simple wills. My most significant cases were real estate matters. While waiting for my bar examination results I earned my real estate salesman's license and attempted to sell real estate. I sold a total of one house to a buddy of mine. My broker was a World War II veteran who was creative in getting loans for nontraditional buyers. After I started my practice he steered real estate closings to me. Two memorable closings required special handling. I had to go to the clients, because they could not come to my office. The broker had helped an elderly lady secure special Federal Housing Authority (FHA) funding. I arrived at her old house in South Richmond and met my client, who appeared to be in her seventies, and her special-needs son, who appeared to be in his fifties. The shack sat in front of some railroad tracks and was formerly in Chesterfield County before the area was annexed by the City of Richmond in the early 1970s. It sat along a busy road that I had frequently traveled. The old house was in rough shape and the lighting consisted of a single light bulb hanging from the ceiling in the kitchen. The old lady was excited over buying her first home, which was located across the road from her in a modest subdivision. It could have just as well been on the other side of the state, because she had little contact with the world outside of her rundown home.

After signing the papers she thanked me. "Mista, I wanna tank you for my new house. This be the first time I ever had indoor plumbing." Winning the lottery would have had less value to her than her new house with indoor plumbing. But I was perplexed. I had traveled this road twice daily going to work at Philip Morris and never noticed these shacks along the tracks. In addition, I was on the road weekly taking Chris to Boy Scout meetings and monthly going to the Army Reserve Center, passing right by the place but never noticing it. Obviously the house with its crude electrical service, wood stove and no plumbing was there all the time. But I had never paid attention to the little shacks. I was disturbed by my own insensitivity to things right in front of me. Poverty and those in need surround us but we somehow fail to see them. Or do we see them and elect to ignore them? I was disappointed with myself for my own blindness and ignorance.

Richmond's McGuire Veterans Hospital was close to the old lady's house. I had seen the new modern brick hospital replace the old World War II era wooden structure with its long corridors connecting the buildings. I had been inside the hospital several times before as a courtesy to my old clients who solicited my help. I was summoned on two occasions to prepare deathbed wills for World War II veterans. They were my brothers and sisters in arms as we shared the kinship of the U.S. Army. This time I entered the spinal cord injury ward to see my new client. Spinal cord injuries are among the most devastating and immobilizing. The realtor had secured a Veterans Administration (VA) loan for my client, and I conducted the closing at his hospital bed. His world was restricted to a gurney and his condition was never going to improve. He had purchased a modest home in the same subdivision in which the real estate broker and I lived, close to the VA Hospital. I wondered how he was going to take care of himself in his home, because he was without a family. But he had a plan to make the quality of his life and that of others better. I noticed the house being modified for handicap accessibility, and a specialized van showed up courtesy of the Veterans Administration. He had struck a deal with a nursing assistant to live there and take care of him in exchange for her getting the house upon his death. He was forever out of the impersonal institutional facility and in a modest home with a yard, grass, and flowers. The nursing assistant received a secure place where she and her son could live at the modest cost of helping to improve the quality of the veteran's life. I learned that compassion and caring, combined with creativity, can accomplish much.

The effective use of time is a lawyer's biggest challenge as he races to meet deadlines and get from one courthouse to another. After cutting my law teeth in Richmond I ventured out to the country. By then I had handled every type of criminal case from shoplifting to capital murder. During my travels around the state I had spotted some quieter places of interest to me. I relocated to Southside Virginia, where tobacco still reigned as king. I moved to South Hill in Mecklenburg County with its two huge lakes, Kerr Lake and Lake Gaston, and abundant recreational areas. Also, my life situation had now changed, and I felt that I had found my thrill (someone special) in South Hill. More on that later.

In the rural community there is a different style of practicing law. It is gentler; more laid back, more genteel, more gentlemanly. Lawyers from the big city demanding formalities like discovery were quickly reminded that "we don't do that around here." All that has since changed, and city and country lawyers now play by the same rule book because of the presence of full-time prosecutors. Though it is easy to lapse into the comfort of informality, you lose your edge by doing so. It is better to follow the prescribed rule book. I stuck to the Judge Wright Rule of always being prepared and trying not to be an embarrassment to the profession. I started out renting an office on the second floor of an old building in downtown South Hill, with its three blocks of storefront buildings. It didn't take long to get on the court appointment list for criminal cases and attract new clients once folks discovered there was a new guy in town doing bankruptcy work. I hired a part-time secretary, Therese, who soon became full time and the bedrock of my practice. We have worked together as a team for a quarter century now. During the peak of my practice I employed four ladies.

A year later I purchased an older house on East Atlantic Street along the main traffic corridor, U.S. Highway 58. I moved my office into it on the first floor and lived there on the second floor. I handled mostly criminal and bankruptcy matters. Our longtime Commonwealth's Attorney retired and his assistant moved up to replace him. I nabbed the part-time position of Assistant Commonwealth Attorney for Mecklenburg County. I usually handled the misdemeanors in Juvenile Court and General District Court, with my boss tackling the felonies in Circuit Court, Virginia's court of record. I also handled all the prison cases from our two correctional facilities, the Mecklenburg Correctional Center and Baskerville Correctional Center (Camp 4). Prison cases have a unique character of their own. Inmates with long sentences are prone to test the correctional system. They can be creative in making or securing contraband such as weapons, alcohol, and drugs. For example, fruit or raisins can be distilled into liquor, and getting drugs smuggled in is not uncommon. There were always fights and assaults to deal with. Inmates cherish a day outside the wire, and some would commit crimes just to get a street charge and a trip to the courthouse for trial. To me it seemed more effective to give inmates institutional charges for petty infractions. The administrative punishment was more immediate and effective. This punishment could include the loss of "good time," which delayed parole eligibility, isolation, and the loss of privileges and jobs. Street charges, on the other hand, just added time to sentences, and after a while time had no meaning. I elected to review the cases the prisons wanted to prosecute as street charges. Assaults on staff were always prosecuted. The inmates liked to concoct a foul mixture of feces and urine to throw on staff and targeted their faces between the forehead and chin. The preferred strike zone was the eyes and mouth areas.

Inmates have their own code of conduct, which includes jailhouse justice, in which, rather than snitching to the authorities, they address their grievances among themselves. Feuding factions square off at an opportune moment to mete out their style of justice using weapons called "shanks," which are homemade knives crafted from a piece of rigid metal, plastic, or wood. Though usually jailbirds don't sing, that is, testify against each other, I remember one occasion when the jailbird did sing. The large open recreation yard in the Mecklenburg Correctional Center had to be subdivided into several smaller exercise areas (rec cages) to cut down on inmate-on-inmate violence. So inmates were locked in the smaller cages for recreation. One inmate was so determined to get to his enemy that he dug under the fence to get to him and managed to put a shank in him several times before the guards could get there to unlock the cage and rescue him. The assailant had his digging timed perfectly so he could not be seen by the officer in the observation tower. He had managed to ease under the fence and stuck a shank in his adversary before the guards could respond.

My most memorable inmate case was that of a man I will call Johnnie C, who was a true lifer. He was convicted of a number of murders and had multiple natural life sentences without parole. He was infamous because of a creative escape attempt. He convinced the sheriff of one of our southwestern counties, whose brother had been killed, that he knew the location of the body of his murdered sibling. Arrangements were made to transport Johnnie to the supposed location. However, Johnnie had a pistol planted there, and after poking around in the woods awhile retrieved the pistol and had an old-fashioned shootout with the officers. He was wounded and the escape attempt was spoiled. Johnnie prided himself on causing trouble in prison. Once he engaged in a "jailhouse romance" with an overweight, unattractive, mildly retarded, lonely, and gullible woman. Part of the prison culture is for inmates to meet lonely women and pretend they are in love with them. The inmate then uses the woman for favors such as money, gifts, pornography, and drugs. Some women will do anything to foster a relationship.

Johnnie convinced the woman that he loved her. After several visits she agreed to smuggle a weapon into the maximum security Mecklenburg Correctional Center. Following Johnnie's instructions she purchased a derringer-style pistol and broke it into two parts and wrapped them in plastic wrap. She secreted them in her female body cavity just as instructed. She successfully made it through security and passed the weapon to Johnnie's mule (another inmate hired to transport contraband in his body cavity). Johnnie's mule placed the items up his rectum and made it through security. The plan was successfully executed.

After leaving the prison the woman arrived at the South Hill bus station too late to catch her bus. The bus station was near the South Hill Police Station, and one of the local police officers noticed her and engaged her in conversation. Eventually she confided in the officer that she felt bad because she had done something wrong and gave the details of her involvement in the delivery of the weapon to the correctional center. One phone call to the prison nabbed the mule with the contraband still in place in his rectum. The derringer was removed from his body cavity and he and Johnnie were prosecuted. Johnnie represented himself during his jury trial and boastfully testified, claiming responsibility for the whole thing, and challenged the jury to give him the maximum sentence allowable. The jury obliged him with the maximum sentence. Johnnie enjoyed the opportunity to mock the system. Johnnie C eventually died in prison.

After eight years as the assistant prosecutor I came to realize that our criminal justice system is actually a system of mostly recycling the same bad actors, first in Juvenile Court, then in the adult system. After a while the faces are familiar and you see the generational connections as the parents accompanying their kids to Juvenile Court one day are the defendants in adult court the next day. Soon you know the family history. It's usually the same old pathetic behavior: fighting, stealing, drinking, and drug use. Behavioral scientists argue that bad behavior is environmentally induced. Maybe so, but surely there is a need for personal accountability.

Our criminal justice systems only survive because of a time-honed system that relies on the willingness of people to admit their guilt, receive their punishment, and move on. Negotiated pleas, or plea bargains, are also absolutely essential, although District Attorneys and Commonwealth Attorneys running for re-election campaign against them and promise a jury trial for everything, which is ridiculous. Our legal system would be paralyzed without the efficiency afforded by assembly-line justice, the system of handling routine cases and promptly dispensing "justice", which I define as a result acceptable to society and the accused. Most criminals want their matters disposed of with the best deal available. The drama plays out daily in courtrooms around the country, with large numbers of accused persons, usually young black, brown, yellow, and tan men standing behind their public defenders or court appointed lawyers on one side of the courtroom, and with the law enforcement officers, witnesses, and victims standing behind the assistant prosecutor an the other side of the courtroom steering people through the system under the watchful eyes of judges and court personnel.

Most criminals know the deal because they have been there before. Sometimes what happens in court looks like a cattle drive to the uninformed public. We have an assembly-line criminal court system that, much like any assembly line, runs smoothly until something has to receive special handling, maybe a custom order. We have a method for dealing with special handling called a trial, where an accused can require the government to prove its allegations beyond a reasonable doubt to gain a criminal conviction. Special orders, however, cost more in the marketplace and in the legal system. On occasion new law school students, social scientists and first-time observers cry foul over the statistical inequities for minorities and poor folks. And in this country you get what you pay for. Actually you may not get all that you pay for, but you are required to pay for what you get.

The problem in most legal arenas is that most indigent folks are unused to paying for what they get from society and are therefore unable to appreciate the value of the professional assistance they receive. They are often people who have not experienced the value of work and have avoided taking personal responsibility for most things. For example, public defenders and court appointed lawyers carry the burden of representing the bulk of criminal defendants. Defendants often voice their displeasure with their appointed lawyers and clamor for "a real lawyer." They tell the judges that they just met their lawyer in the hallway right before the trial of their misdemeanor case. But they don't disclose that they failed to keep their appointment in the lawyer's office because they didn't have a ride, a baby sitter, or it was too hot or too cold for them. The judge reminds them that they can hire any lawyer they choose and offers a continuance to hire another lawyer. They mumble a little and then accept the deal as offered and the judge moves on to the next case. There are sentencing guidelines for felony convictions in the federal and most state court systems that scientifically determine the range of punishment to be handed out. Convicted felons receive a score based upon their entire life's worth. Factors such as previous convictions, education, employment history, family stability, marital status, military service, addictions, and the support of one's dependents weigh into the numerical score that is then converted to a sentencing range. Obviously those with positive backgrounds make out better that those with excuses. In Virginia, young people of color usually constitute the majority of the criminal defendant population even in communities where they constitute the smaller percentage of the population at large. They will recite the traditional laundry lists of excuses for their behavior: single mom home, absentee father, poor education, and lack of employment right before they are sentenced and confined in our jails and prisons. This is not to suggest that being arrested equates to guilt. Recently my faith in the criminal justice system was reaffirmed.

I represented a juvenile who was charged with felonious wounding and shooting into an occupied motor vehicle. He was arrested and held in juvenile detention because of his previous juvenile convictions and because he had been suspended from high school as the result of pending assault charges against school staff members. He appeared to be my typical juvenile defendant. He had a criminal history, came from a single parent home, and lacked interest in his education as demonstrated by poor school grades. The prosecutor elected to try him as an adult because he was over age 15 and met the criteria to be tried as an adult. His mother was adamant that he was innocent and wanted to hire me after his case was shuffled between two court-appointed lawyers. His previous lawyer was successful in getting him released from detention and placed on house arrest.

I took the case with reluctance because the Northern Virginia venue was unfamiliar and nearly 200 miles away. When I met my client in his home he offered little in terms of specifics concerning his case. However, when his mother arrived home she supplied me with detailed information concerning her son's every move the night of the alleged incident. She had real names of witnesses and a detailed ledger tracing her son's movements on that night. Her theory was that a snitch fabricated a story to take the heat off himself on an unrelated matter. The victim did not know who shot him and the state's star witness was absent at the initial court date. The snitch had been released from juvenile detention in exchange for his cooperation and seemed to have disappeared. The court granted the Commonwealth's Attorney motion for a continuance for the felony and tried two assault cases that were still pending against my client. Present with my client were his mother and his father, who came in from New York. I was impressed by the family support. I knew what the deal was, having played the prosecutorial game before. In the criminal world it is quid pro quo, something for something: you give something to get something. The snitch had evidently played his get-out-of-jail card in exchange for his fabricated story. He then apparently recanted his story to the police and did not show up for the next court date. The felony charges against my client were therefore dropped. What makes this case significant to me is the parental involvement with their son. The single mom actively monitored her son's moves and the father was present to offer support to his son at a critical time.

After three decades in the law business I have matured enough to accept the concept that confinement solely for the sake of punishment is acceptable. I've come to this conclusion based on playing the various roles in the courtroom of defense attorney, prosecutor, and substitute judge. I agree that it is preferable to exercise alternative options such as education, rehabilitation, and vocational training. At one time Virginia had prison farms for raising food for inmates and furniture shops supplying items to government offices. But American entrepreneurship took over and the care and feeding of inmates has become big business. Virginia even overbuilt her prisons and offered excess bed space to other states, such as Connecticut and Texas. Outside money rolled in. The charter buses rolled in from the north and south with families traveling long distances to visit their inmates and spending money locally. Private prisons now dot the countryside because there is money in human warehousing.

Prisons, which we now call Correctional Centers, bring cash to communities. Prison guards, now called correctional officers, have job security, make a good wage, and retire after 20 years. Farm boys leave the fields and work in climate-controlled facilities. Community colleges offer courses and degrees marketing confinement skills. Corrections spell cash to rural communities. Every county in Southside Virginia has at least one Correctional Center – correction: prison, because no correction takes place, only confinement. Mecklenburg County held the distinction of opening the state's first modern prison in the early 1970s. Mecklenburg Correctional Center was designed to hold the state's worst actors and death row inmates in maximum security. It housed the state's electric chair. But it was fallible. Two death row inmates from Richmond, James and Linwood Briley: the "Briley Brothers", planned and executed a daring escape from death row and stayed on the run for a long time. They hid in plain view on the streets of Philadelphia until eventually captured at a barbecue. Linwood Briley was my former client and my first capital murder case.

I have gone to jail and prison many times and fortunately was released after brief stays. It started with the Richmond City Jail and the Virginia State Penitentiary known as "Spring Street." It then progressed to other places of confinement around the state. I wasn't an inmate, just a defense lawyer visiting my clients. I recall a memorable jailhouse visit to my client in the Rockingham County Jail in Harrisonburg, Virginia, in the early 1980s. Harrisonburg is in the picturesque Shenandoah Valley. I called ahead to check on visiting hours. I went inside the aged facility to arrange a meeting with my client. I was instructed to go outside to the rear of the jail and stand by the fence. My client was brought out to the tiny fenced-in space that served as a recreational area and visiting place. We talked through the fence. But it beat my visits to Spring Street, the original 19th century Virginia State Penitentiary in Richmond on the main traffic corridor of U.S. Highway 1. At Spring Street you entered through a series of large security gates locked manually behind you and had to be escorted through the center of the inside area (the yard), and then locked in a building while you waited for your client. I will always remember Spring Street, which has now been torn down, because when I was a kid we passed by it every time we went to Virginia. The inmates were always banging on bars and cursing. Dad would admonish us to behave or else we could wind up there. That message was reinforced during our summer stints in Nottoway County as we watched inmates from nearby prison camps working on the roads.

Judges must show restraint and patience as they hear legal arguments and pleas for leniency. They have usually already heard it all. In the end there are few surprises, because you know what to expect and have told your client to bring the appropriate underwear, shower shoes, and toothbrush for the anticipated jail sentence. The unspoken truth is that sometimes our jails are places of refuge, much like the train stations and bus stations that used to be open all the time. Jails tend to fill up in the winter and thin out in the spring, because inmates get three hot meals and a cot. Sheriffs get paid based on their inmate population and all is well.

I serve as a substitute judge and special justice at the convenience of the court. When I sit as judge I am usually receptive to creative sentences, but I want defense counsel to give me something I can say yes to. And don't deal me a hand of excuse cards. It is hard for me to accept idleness and joblessness. In my community seasonal agricultural jobs go begging as able-bodied men stand on street corners looking for handouts. Mexican guest workers arrive every spring. Hotel Mexicano, a charter bus, stops at the South Hill Wal-Mart to drop the workers off and returns in the fall for the trip back to Mexico. In six months imported workers usually earn enough money to provide for their families for a year or better. Guest workers have to be paid more as a penalty for not hiring Americans. But where are the local workers? Where are the chain-smoking, able-bodied men who could be working in the fields cultivating the crop they are addicted to? I have also seen construction job opportunities begging for workers.

I am willing to accept a less-than-perfect legal system because I know that prosecutors, defense attorneys, and judges genuinely strive to keep the criminal justice system functional. In my opinion part of the solution for making the system better is to increase the diversity of assistant prosecutors. The assistant DA, using TV terms, is the most critical player in the system. Prosecutors strike the deals, can take charges off the plate, and get creative sentences approved. Judges are conservative beings and are selected to uphold the law. Judges hear the evidence and apply the law accordingly. Judges usually follow the recommendations of the good guy, the prosecutor, the DA, not some defense attorney singing the Poor Client Blues.

Increasing the population of assistant prosecutors of color will require monumental attitude changes. Our youth must look favorably on the roles of police officers, prosecutors, and probation officers, and want to become them.

When I assumed the role of Assistant Commonwealth Attorney I was reminded by the newly retired Commonwealth Attorney that prosecutors are there to help people. That was a profound statement as to the power held by a prosecutor. I finally came to realize what he meant. Helping is not caving in, but craftsmanship. Craft something that is going to help victims, defendants, and the community when appropriate. Have a high-profile defendant caught speeding recklessly down the highway perform community service in the hospital or schools as part of the punishment. Help the right youngsters keep their criminal records clean so they can be eligible to join the military or police force later on. Most judges fully appreciate the temptations of youth to experiment with alcohol and drugs. .

I endorse the concept of firm, immediate, escalating punishment. Once convicted a person should do what is required right away, whether it be reporting for confinement or performing community service. First-time offenders should be given a second chance for small acts like shoplifting or passing bad checks, provided they promptly make restitution. Above all the guilty should reflect upon their behavior and bad decisions in a controlled environment such as monitored house arrest or in confinement.

Unfortunately, like most well-meaning parents I failed my child by not heeding sound advice early on. I bailed him out of his first speeding ticket and protected him from being charged with unauthorized use of a motor vehicle when he took someone's car and went joyriding. As a result of leniency he wrapped his mother's car around a telephone pole on his next unauthorized venture. Fortunately he wasn't hurt and we thought he had learned a valuable lesson. We were wrong. When he went to college and learned to kite checks, I struck deals with the local merchants when the checks bounced. With two professional parents and exposure to world travel, he had wanted to be a dentist, but opted to be a career defendant instead. After spending most of his adult life in prisons in Maryland and Virginia he promised that his last incarceration was going to be the final one when his grandmother visited him. I had to push her in a wheelchair for the visit.

We picked him up from the correctional center on his mother's 55th birthday. He was anxious to go and immediately threw his prison garb in the trash. He had a choice of living in two nice homes and had a car and two job opportunities waiting. He had the love and support of his family and settled into his new home with a bedroom with private bath overlooking the river. He started a job as an apprentice HVAC technician. But then he started getting high instead of going to work. Within six months he was in residential drug rehab and was released on Christmas Eve. He spent his first Christmas in many years outside a prison in a warm and cozy home. His parents went to the AA and NA meetings with him and his peer counselors offered him support. His employer took him back and a bank lent him money for a car, which he promptly wrecked. But a used car salesman helped him purchase another one. Then the bad check notices started to come in, followed by the delinquent notices from the bank. He stopped working, eating, and taking care of himself. He was getting high and that was all that mattered. He was ordered to leave the house and the car was repossessed. He tried rehab again but was kicked out for failure to follow the rules. Because he was on the streets of Richmond, we purchased him a membership at the downtown YMCA so he could bathe. We lost all contact with him until he was arrested in the neighboring county. The state prosecuted him for drugs. The federal government prosecuted him for mail fraud and identity theft.

We were relieved to know that he was alive. Everyone had had enough. Shortly before his fortieth birthday the federal judge wanted to go above the sentencing guidelines because his elaborate scheme of mail fraud and identity theft had wreaked havoc on many lives. But the judge was bound by the guidelines because of a deal, a plea agreement that didn't allow for an upward departure from the guidelines. The judge handed out the stiffest punishment he could under the agreement. We watched. Thank God he was alive.

What addiction is so strong that it will make the strong weak, the rich poor, and cause people to abandon everything and everyone because of its power? It is what made one of my favorite female vocalists live on the street and sell her body for another hit. It is so powerful that the United States Congress made the penalty for selling it many times higher that its sister in powder form. On the street it is called smack, crack, or crack cocaine. Small-time dealers can cultivate a flock of loyal customer by giving it away free until the client gets hooked and then must have it at any cost.

We share the embarrassment, pain, and agony of a child gone wild. What did we do wrong? The answer is nothing. Each of us is responsible for our decisions. We have no control over another person. If anything, as parents we didn't let go and let God soon enough. That's tough but essential. I remember seeing a letter to Christopher from a fellow inmate who wrote, "Perhaps your problem is your well intended benevolent parents who provided for you too well and protected you too much. You are not of the stock of us who had nothing, saw nothing and did nothing. Yet you complain without accepting responsibility for you own actions. Grow up man." As parents we need to let our children grow up and deal with the consequences of their actions early on.

CHAPTER EIGHT

THE HARVEST

Geese fly in a V formation to create an updraft for the flock. The unified effort makes it easier for the flock to fly. They work in concert as a coordinated team. Should one goose become tired, sick, or injured and fall out of formation two others will follow it to the ground and stick with him until he regains the strength to rejoin the flock or to join another flock.

We can learn team work from geese. If we work as a team we can accomplish more than as individuals. Business requires discipline and teamwork. We usually need to partner with like-minded individuals to achieve our goals. Patience is absolutely essential in business. And one must be able to wait for a return. It is like planting seeds and waiting for the harvest. It is important for us to invest in our future. Such requires financial training and discipline. We should start with giving to our local church or charity. Then a portion of our earnings should be invested or saved for future needs. Unless we plant financial seeds there will be no harvest of emergency funds or retirement income.

My interest in real estate made it a logical choice for a business venture. Joseph Riggs, my Hull Street neighbor, owned a lot of real estate that he was trying to get rid of. It was mostly junk property that he had intended to renovate but lost interest in. Mr. Riggs offered me some of his aging investment property. My first business partner LeRoi Templeton and I devoted countless hours and energy in an effort to renovate an ornate house a few streets over from my office. The two-story brick monster with 12-foot ceilings, hardwood floors, and thick wood molding had been ravaged by time and neglect. I envisioned it in its former days of glory. However, our limited resources, lack of time, and vandalism eventually dulled our spirits and we abandoned the project and returned the property to Mr. Riggs.

The second time around I partnered with Frank Spencer. We had met in the Army Reserve and he was from neighboring Lunenburg County, where he grew up on a tobacco farm. He had enlisted in the Army out of high school to escape the farm and advance his opportunities. Our strategy was to invest in decent property requiring only cosmetic improvements. Each piece of rental property was spruced up and well maintained. Our initial purchase was in Virginia Beach, not too far from the ocean front. And our other venue was Richmond, where we purchased two condominiums in a good neighborhood facing Forest Hill Park in Southside Richmond. We used self-help for painting, floor refinishing, and minor plumbing when we renovated the properties. For the most part we had good tenants. As a landlord there are constant headaches, such as late rent payments and maintenance. We used our earning to purchase other property and picked up a dilapidated house in the Church Hill section of Richmond at a delinquent tax sale.

The two-story house was in bad shape, and cleaning trash and debris out of the place was a major task. After devoting countless hours to the renovation effort, we realized that, because we had limited time to devote to the project, it was a job better left to professionals. We decided to board the house up until we secured resources to renovate it. Fortunately the once-decaying neighborhood with its stately old houses was making a comeback as investors and developers poured money into the area. The property caught the eye of a developer who owned most of the houses on the block. We sold it and used the profit to satisfy the debt on our other properties.

We learned some valuable lessons concerning human behavior along the way. First, check on your property frequently. Second, evict tenants early when they misbehave. The lessee in one of our units secretly moved, and allowed a lady with a bunch of foster children to occupy the place. The place was destroyed before we were able to evict her. We entered the door to the once pristine condo to find every inch of floor space covered with trash, clothing, toys, bicycles, broken furniture and debris. You could not see the hardwood floor when you went in the place. Dirty dishes and pots and pans covered the stove and filled the sink, and there was moldy food in the refrigerator. Roaches had taken up permanent residence in the stove and refrigerator, which had to be discarded. The toilet was stopped up and the tub was black with filth. We resumed our day work routine to get the place back into shape. The once nice residence was in shambles by the time we took possession. We discarded everything in the place and we took several truck loads of trash to the city dump to clear the place. The once beautiful hardwood floors had burn spots from dropped cigarettes butts, and had to be refinished. The entire place had to be repainted and the plumbing repaired. We waged a major roach eradication campaign to make the place livable. Though tenant behavior blunted our enthusiasm regarding providing decent affordable housing, we didn't abandon our goal of offering decent housing to those in need.

Real estate is usually a sound investment because it tends to appreciates in value. Our real estate has appreciated in value over time. Because we left our earnings in the business we were able to handle unexpected events such as repairs and special assessments. I have also invested in utility stocks and individual retirement accounts, which when left alone can substantially increase in value. Everyone should take full advantage of employer-sponsored retirement programs and develop their own investment strategy to prepare for the future.

There is no harvest without the planting of seeds. People need to be disciplined with money and invest wisely. I see too many older people relying strictly on Social Security for their needs. We are already on notice that our Social Security system is in jeopardy. It doesn't take much money to build up a nest egg. It takes saving a little consistently over a long period of time. Saving is a foreign concept to most Americans now because of the proliferation of easy credit. Now that America is experiencing an economic calamity we must wake up and cultivate our individual harvest.

PART IV: GENERALSHIP

CHAPTER NINE

WE ARE SOLDIERS TOO

The mission of the Army Reserve is to provide trained units and qualified persons available for active duty.

The Vietnam era Army Reserve was not well respected by the nation and its active duty counterparts. General Abrams, former Army Chief of Staff, attempted to cure the cultural divide by making sure that the American people were inextricably involved in future wars and instituted what is known as the "Abrams Doctrine." Its intent was for the entire nation to be involved in America's wars by closely tying the reserve component to all future military operations. Therefore a significant number of functions were transferred to the Army Reserve, as the military was downsized following the Vietnam War. The active component was usually responsible for the training and readiness of the reserve component. There was often friction between the active component "big brother" types and the less respected reservists, who were relegated to the back seat. Big brother thought he knew best. That changed after the Gulf War, when the reserve component played a critical role in the short campaign. With the downsizing of our military, many soldiers joined the reserves after leaving active duty.

The Army Reserve has a culture of its own. I attended my first inactive duty training session, called a drill assembly or simply "drill," on a Tuesday night. At that time the 80th Division Headquarters was conducting its drills on two weekday nights and one Saturday, which was an inefficient way to conduct business. We met in a large assembly hall, and a collection of veterans of World War II, Korea, and Vietnam filled the ranks along with their fellow reservists, many of whom had not served a tour of active duty. Reservists represented every occupation, profession, and segment of our society, and served for a variety of reasons.

The common denominator was that everyone was a volunteer. Some had served on active duty. Some men had enlisted to avoid the draft and possible service in Vietnam, and wound up liking the Army. Some women were recruited for their civilian-acquired skills and had abbreviated initial training. Some, including me, had joined to earn money to help finance their education. I was feeling out of place in this hodgepodge of imitation soldiers. To me the drill resembled more of a social gathering than military training, as people spent half their time socializing with each other with a little work squeezed between the opening and closing formation. Such was my introduction to the Army Reserve.

After assimilation into the Army Reserve culture I gained a better understanding of the dynamics of the reserve culture. This was the Cold War and numbers meant a lot as NATO (North Atlantic Treaty Organization) stared down the Soviet Union. We maintained massive numbers of units and inflated personnel figures in anticipation of the next world war. Our huge military structure was heavy in reserve units. The Army Reserve had numerous units of various types, usually within fifty miles of most major metropolitan areas.Many reservists spent their entire careers in the same unit rotating to different positions for promotions. There was a self-serve system of personnel management. If you saw an assignment you wanted, you went after it.

The quality of reserve units differed according to the local leadership. I moved to the position of training officer for the 80th Division Headquarters and Headquarters Company, where I assisted the Headquarters Commandant (Commander) with the individual training of soldiers. Job responsibilities included ensuring soldiers received the required military occupational specialty (MOS) training for their positions. Sometimes unit missions would change, requiring the entire unit to be retrained in a new MOS, or individuals sometimes migrated to other units when they relocated to new geographical locations. Others were promoted into positions and were required to retrain. There was a somewhat laissez faire system of MOS training, and some soldiers could qualify by engaging in on-the-job training (OJT). Also there was individual and unit readiness training, including weapons qualification; nuclear, biological, and chemical (NBC) training; and a bunch of required classes: Geneva Convention, standards of conduct; premobilization legal, personal affairs, etc. Training usually had to compete with getting the staff work done, and there was a constant battle to get the colonels to release their soldiers for training. Enlisted soldiers were required to take proficiency tests periodically, and most of them scored badly because of the lack of preparation and enthusiasm. I was able to carve out some fun in the Army Reserve after leaving the division headquarters. I obtained an assignment as company commander in our Training Brigade, which consisted of a bunch of instructors and support staff who provided training to new soldiers at Army training posts like Fort Benning, Georgia, and Fort Jackson, South Carolina. My company met at Fort Lee, Virginia, south of Richmond, and was 150 miles away from its higher headquarters. After motivating my NCOs, we were able to significantly improve the unit and meet Army standards. The key to success was educating everyone on the required standards, getting their buy-in and acceptance of the standards, and the strict enforcement of the standards. Soldiers respond to innovative leadership and being challenged. I left that position to become Training Officer for the Leadership Academy, which was the training unit for drill sergeant candidates. We met at Fort A.P. Hill, Virginia, about forty-five miles north of Richmond. The drill sergeant candidates would receive the bulk of their training at various sites throughout Virginia and finish it at Fort Jackson, South Carolina. Once armed with the traditional drill sergeant campaign hat or Smokey the Bear hat, they were able to wreak havoc on the lives of new privates.

An organized personnel management system within the 80th Division began at the field grade officer level, which is the rank of major. Officers for the first time were involuntarily directed to assignments. I received notice that I was to become the Commandant of the 80th Division Headquarters and Headquarters Company, which meant dealing with the upper echelons of ranking officers, generals, colonels, and lieutenant colonels. I held little affection for the headquarters and was unenthusiastic about returning there. I was reminded by my boss that as a new major I did not have a vote if I wanted a job, and was directed to report as ordered. Much tact and diplomacy was required in the job. I worked for the Chief of Staff, the ranking colonel, who served as a buffer between the colonels and me, and with his support I was able to reinstate Army standards. To conduct the required field readiness training, I was able to move the entire headquarters company to Fort A.P. Hill for three days to perform all our field training at one time instead of in the traditional monthly piecemeal fashion. Also, everyone was required to participate in physical fitness training every month, and take an annual physical fitness test. This was a major change of culture.

Starting in the early 1980s the Reagan administration was able to carve out a robust defense budget. The Army Reserve then began to be challenged concerning readiness and relevance. It had to be trained and ready as programmed. When enhanced training opportunities and better equipment started to arrive, soldiers became more serious about the Army Reserve and commanders became more professional. I left the division headquarters for an assignment with the 80th Maneuver Training Command, which conducted training and evaluations for Army Reserve and Army National Guard units. These units were evaluated on a fixed schedule, and their report card was of grave concern to the commander and higher headquarters. As part of the Infantry Team we traveled extensively, and spent considerable time in the field with the units we evaluated. It was a great job and as close to real Army stuff as one could get, despite trips to places like Fort Stewart, Georgia, and Camp Shelby, Mississippi, in the middle of hot and humid summers. During one such trip to Camp Shelby, one of the National Guard units killed an eight-foot rattlesnake with a twelve-inch girth, which they preserved on ice as a trophy until the exercise was concluded. Then it was fried rattlesnake time.

I managed to complete the Command and General Staff College and get promoted to lieutenant colonel before my next assignment to the 2079th Reserve Forces School as the School Secretary, a combination S1 and S4, responsible for personnel and supply. Reserve Forces Schools were responsible for the conduct of MOS and professional development courses in a designated geographical area. Reserve Forces Schools operated the way satellite campuses do for colleges and had to meet the individual training needs of soldiers in their assigned geographical area. Accreditation was controlled by the proponent TRADOC School, such as Engineer, Military Police, Signal, Transportation, and Quartermaster. The 2079th was populated mainly with retirement-eligible soldiers, many of whom were at the terminal point of their careers. Tending to the personnel and logistical needs of our soldiers spread over the state with only a skeleton staff was rather challenging and required creative management. I was just getting into the swing of things when I was selected for battalion command.

The 1st Battalion, 319th Infantry Regiment, was a training battalion comprised of drill sergeants and cadre located in Lynchburg, Virginia, and 110 miles from my home. Traditionally the battalion conducted basic combat training at Fort Benning, Georgia, and Fort Jackson, South Carolina, and was regarded as one of the premier battalions in the division. My arrival was a surprise to the unit. The previous battalion commander had been promoted to colonel and had moved on. The initial formation was at 1900 hours on a Friday night, and I introduced myself to the battalion and received a cool reception. I conducted an open ranks inspection and met all the soldiers in attendance as I went through the ranks. After that I spent several hours conducting a command and staff meeting with the key leaders. I spelled out my expectations and leadership philosophy.

The weekend proved to be a disaster. Early Saturday morning the dreaded 80th Division Training and Evaluation Team showed up. The team was the Division Commander's eyes and ears regarding training readiness, and a report went directly to him. The battalion failed in all categories: personnel accountability, training management, conduct of training, and training planning. Starting with the opening formation the company First Sergeants were unable to account for all their soldiers. Training was a flop because the instructors were not prepared and the paperwork was not up to standards. Failing this type of evaluation was normally the kiss of death for the commander. Because I was the brand-new guy I temporarily escaped the wrath of my chain of command. There would be an unannounced re-evaluation to determine my fate.

I realized that the battalion usually consolidated all training at battalion level which zapped the company commanders' initiative and accountability. A habitual problem of the Army Reserve was the reliance on too few people doing most of the work as the majority simply looked on. Thereafter we conducted training at the company level, which required the thorough development of more soldiers. We were able to pull things together using detailed training meetings before each training assembly, so that when the 80th Division Training and Evaluation Team conducted its reevaluation everything was in order and we passed with flying colors.

Our assigned annual training mission was at Fort Benning, Georgia, where we would shadow the active duty battalion in the conduct of basic combat training. I was confident we were prepared for the mission since we had meticulously prepared for it. However, our performance did not match our preparation, as my subordinate leaders and drill sergeants could not stand up under the pressure of eighteen-hour workdays and the hot and humid July Georgia heat, especially since we were housed in old World War II wooden barracks without air conditioning, with second-floor temperatures exceeding 100 degrees. We did, however, manage to improve significantly during the latter part of the mission. I was puzzled by the lack of consistency in our performance and the colossal failure of junior leaders to function independently. This was a leadership challenge resident in the Army Reserve, where young leaders sometimes lack experience and maturity as a result of having few opportunities to lead on a long-term basis. There was one other disguised dynamic. Individuals stayed in their jobs too long and lacked freshness.

The following year our mission was at Fort Jackson, South Carolina. I reshuffled the battalion by rotating leaders into other companies and battalion staff, thus infusing new blood throughout the battalion. We then began an intensive train-up for the next mission by training, rehearsing, self-evaluation (after action review), and then retraining and re-evaluation. Our slice of the Fort Jackson mission included the field training exercise, which was the culmination of basic combat training skills, and graduation. If you don't like the springtime weather in Columbia, South Carolina, you just wait because it will change. We reported there in late March to miserable cold and damp weather during the time in the field. By graduation day we were out of field jackets and parkas and in short sleeves. This mission was a complete success with everything done nearly to perfection. The battalion had redeemed itself and regained its reputation as one of the best in the division. I was having too much fun, so I was moved to the 2nd Brigade Headquarters, Salem, Virginia, as the Brigade Executive Officer, with primary responsibility for staff functions.

I was directed by my superiors to apply for the Army War College, which is the Army's highest senior service school. I shared with them that I was tired of school and was not interested in the Army War College, at which time I was ordered to apply. I was accepted for the U.S. Army War College Class of 1995. Senior Service School at the Army War College, or its equivalent, is a master's degree level program. Graduates usually enhance their chance of being promoted to the rank of colonel and selection for brigade level command. The War College operated two programs – the resident and distance learning programs. The distance learning, or correspondence, program took two years to complete, and each year consisted of 10 months of individual work at home followed by a two-week session at the Army War College in Carlisle, Pennsylvania.

The distance learning course was a grueling individual grind that sometimes overwhelmed its participants, who had to do the course work in addition to their Army Reserve job, civilian job, and family obligations. Each year there were about 10 papers on various topics that had to be submitted on a prescribed schedule. Time discipline and an enduring work ethic were required. Each spring a dreaded box of reading material arrived. It was up to the student to digest it and submit the required papers, ranging from leadership to strategic operations. I dedicated the very early morning and late evenings for my studies.

The early part of the day was conducive to reading, leaving the remainder of the day to reflect upon the readings and make notes to myself. I purchased a personal computer and moved into the modern age of information management. I attempted to close each day out with putting my thoughts on the day's readings in writing. I promised myself that come hell or high water I would submit all my papers on time. As the submission date neared I completed each required paper and submitted all papers on time, having to race to the mailbox on a few occasions to get them postmarked by the date they were due. We always received our submissions back with the instructor's comments in the margins. A few of my papers resembled my freshman English compositions, with red ink comments all over them. I think the War College aided in my selection to colonel, which I viewed as the culminating point of my military career. After all, my severance from the Army was more than 20 years overdue.

When I got promoted, there were few opportunities for new colonels. I was accepted on the General Staff as the Division G3 Operations Officer, and applied for a colonel-level command. Those desiring command assignments could apply for them twice a year and their records went before a competitive board of officers who made the selections. I was selected for assignment at the Commandant 2079 Reserve Forces School. The Army Reserve was undergoing restructuring and the Reserve Forces Schools were being phased out, so my tenure was going to be short. The 2079th harbored many of the same old soldiers who were just trying to compile enough time to retire. Many were overweight or unproductive. I used my newness to crash old alliances and challenged each individual's commitment to the Army Reserve. Their options were to become productive soldiers, retire, or transfer to Individual Ready Reserve (IRR), known as the control group, a vast pool of individual soldiers opting out of troop unit programs.

After reviewing the results of our Army Physical Fitness Test (APFT), I noted the conspicuous lack of participation by some individuals. Upon inquiry I discovered that some soldiers held physical profiles, which is a temporary excuse from some form of physical activity, and used them as a permanent excuse. However, permanent physical limitations could disqualify soldiers for further service, or at least limited their career fields. This was a medical determination for medical evaluation boards to decide. I huddled my leaders together and we scrutinized the records of all soldiers holding profiles. They were then counseled individually regarding wellness, physical fitness, and nutrition as we discussed their individual situations. I challenged them to adjust their lifestyles for their own sake and not for the Army, and assured them that we genuinely cared about them. After all, the Army saves retirement money whenever someone dies prematurely. Most were just lazy and needed a boost to get them motivated. I corralled all the soldiers with physical profiles into one group and assigned an enthusiastic former First Sergeant as their leader, with the mission of mentoring them. They dubbed themselves "F Troop" and made their own banner which was prominently displayed. Over the course of six months they were getting healthy, passing the AFPT, and participating in field training. I was pleased to see the soldiers respond favorably. One soldier thanked me for saving him from a life of potential obesity. I knew my tenure as School Commandant would be brief because all the schools were being reorganized. So I competed for another assignment.

I was reassigned as the Commander of the 7th Brigade (Training Support), 80th Division (Training), in Salem, Virginia. Our slogan was: "An Opportunity to Excel: No Complaining, Sniveling, or Whimpering." Subordinate units were dispersed throughout Virginia. Shortly thereafter I was selected as the Assistant Division Commander (Support), the third in command of the 80th Division. I then set my sights on retirement with thirty years of service, which is the customary maximum time of service authorized for colonels. Every fall a competitive general officer selection board meets, and qualified colonels could apply for consideration to be promoted to brigadier general. I had submitted my application several times before. Because I was nearing my thirty-year mark, I planned my retirement picnic. Then I received a telephone call from Major General Bambrough, the Deputy Commanding General of the U.S. Army Reserve Command, congratulating me on my selection for brigadier general, subject to Congressional approval.

I was selected for the unannounced position as the Assistant Division Commander (Operations) for 80th Division (Institutional Training), Richmond, Virginia, which was vacated by my War College classmate and mentor Charles Wilson, who was selected as Commander of the 98th Division (Institutional Training), Rochester, New York, a two-star command. Charles (Chuck) Wilson and I met at the war College. He was our class president and presented himself as a no-nonsense, straight-shooting guy. He was born in Atlanta, Georgia, but raised in Detroit, Michigan. He provides a great example of the American dream. He had a good job at General Motors after high school and was enjoying his new convertible when he was drafted into the Army. After a stint in Vietnam he joined the Detroit Police Department, earned his bachelor's degree, and rose to head the Department. He was later selected to be the Chief of the Fire Department and the Head of Safety for Detroit.

Unlike qualified active duty colonels who are all considered for promotion to brigadier general, qualified reserve colonels must apply annually for general officer positions in the Army Reserve. There were approximately one hundred general officer positions. An announcement was distributed each spring listing the anticipated vacancies and applicants could compete for a number of the advertised positions and also for a position that was not advertised, because unanticipated vacancies were not uncommon. The general officer selection procedure is the most scrutinized process in the Army. Every entry in the officer's official record must be validated and verified by documentation. Even minor criminal or serious driving infractions, income tax, or financial issues can derail a candidate. The civilians and NCOs in the General Officer Management Branch who finalize the packets can detect even the slightest discrepancies. Army acronyms were not acceptable, and every entry had to be presented in plain English. It took several phone calls and multiple corrections for me to make my records acceptable.

The number of general officers serving at any given time is strictly limited, and actual promotion dates lag behind Senate confirmation by as much as twelve to eighteen months. I was fortunate in having only a nine-month wait. My long-time mentor and Division Commander, Major General Jamie Brower, presided over the promotion. The ceremony was attended by many of my family members and a host of 80th Division soldiers and civilians, many of whom had mentored and encouraged me to take assignments and apply for opportunities, in some of which I had been frankly uninterested. But they had pushed me well beyond my comfort zone and self-imposed limitations. It often takes other people with a wider vision to recognize our potential and push us beyond the security of our limited vision.

The first stop along the path to brigadier general is the Brigadier General Orientation Course, or Charm School, as it is called. It is mandatory for all brigadier general nominees and their spouses. We were sequestered at Fort Leavenworth, Kansas, maybe as a reminder of the penalty for misconduct, since the Army Disciplinary Barracks was in plain view. There is much to be learned when ascending to the general officer world. Being a general officer is a somewhat privileged position, with people vying for your attention. There are also tremendous responsibilities. We were admonished not to let the position go to our heads because there was zero tolerance for misconduct or unethical behavior. We heard from all the generals on the Army Staff in the Pentagon. Everyone sat up and paid close attention to the remarks by the Judge Advocate General (JAG) and the Inspector General (IG), who made it clear that, despite all the warnings, some generals managed to get into trouble. The course was hosted by General Eric Shinseki, Chief of Staff of the Army. He was the Army's most senior leader. General Shinseki is a straight-shooting, tell-it-like-it-is kind of guy.

As the Assistant Division Commander (Operations), I was the second in command, with the primary responsibility for training and operations. I traveled extensively, visiting training and making sure things progressed as planned. It was a fast-paced job that demanded most of my time, which is common for most general officers in the Army Reserve. Most wind up retiring from their civilian jobs or putting them on hold so they can meet the demands of the Army. As a result I had to cut back on my law practice to devote the requisite time to the position. I was traveling all over the country coordinating training, securing resources, and attending meetings and conferences.

I was also selected to serve on the Army Reserve Forces Policy Committee (ARFPC), which was a panel of Army Reserve and Army National Guard general officers who advised the Secretary of the Army on reserve component matters. The ARFPC usually met quarterly in the Pentagon. Our quarterly meetings normally started with a secret operational briefing on the Army's worldwide missions. Then we were updated on new developments and the progress of former projects from the last meeting. The final product was supposed to be our briefing to the Secretary of the Army. However, our best efforts to candidly advise the Secretary of the Army were hampered by the Pentagon mentality that the locals know best. The locals were the Army officers and civilians who worked in the Pentagon and influenced the flow of information to and from the ARFPC. Nothing controversial was ever to get by them. Near the conclusion of each meeting the Assistant Secretary of the Army for Manpower and Reserve Affairs met with us to review our final work product. Then the painful process of reviewing our briefing slides took place. Usually every word had to be tweaked for political and military correctness. I found the whole process to be frustrating and gained a better appreciation of why a bureaucracy perpetuates itself and seldom changes. The out-briefings were always attended by the Vice Chief of Staff of the Army, who actually ran the Army Staff, and members of the Army Staff. During my tenure the Secretary of the Army was usually not in attendance because of other commitments.

CHAPTER TEN

IROQUOIS WARRIORS

Once I was eligible for consideration for promotion to the grade of major general I applied for other assignments at that grade, including assignments to anticipated vacancies, as well as unannounced assignments. The selection process is secretive and the results are not published for several months following the meeting of the selection board that convenes each fall. One evening I received a phone call from MG Bambrough, Deputy Commanding General of the U.S. Army Reserve Command, congratulating me on my selection to command the 98th Division (Institutional Training). The position was occupied by my mentor MG Charles Wilson, who was selected to succeed MG Bambrough as the Deputy Commanding General of the Army Reserve Comand. Again I was selected for an unanticipated opportunity, and twice followed in the big footsteps of one of the great mentors of reserve officers.

I assumed command of the 98th Division (Institutional Training) on August 2, 2002, in Rochester, New York. The Army was going through a major transformation, and the Army Reserve was being radically converted from a strategic reserve to an operational reserve. It was essential for everyone to understand Army Transformation. Our units were located in an eight-state region, including Maine, New Hampshire, Vermont, Massachusetts, Connecticut, Rhode Island, New York, and New Jersey. I sensed that tradition was fully entrenched in the division's culture and change was not welcomed, because the change of command ceremony was conducted indoors on a hot August day. We wore Army Greens, the dress uniform, instead of our work uniform, called BDUs (battle dress uniform). When I inquired as to why we were indoors, I was told that it was a tradition for the division. The reason it was a tradition for the division was that all the previous change of command ceremonies had taken place in March, a time of year during which Rochester's climate made it necessary to schedule events indoors. But now it was August, and nobody cared to change.

The Opening Act: Change of Command

Soldiers, Families, Friends, Neighbors:

I have received the colors of the 98th Division from a great soldier, a great American, and mentor, Major General Charles Wilson. I accept the challenge of commanding the Iroquois Division. I can't tell you how I got here. But it's been a wonderful journey. I thank God for guiding my path. After doing time in one of our institutions to the southeast, it was my intention upon my release some thirty-two years ago to exit the Army ASAP. Instead I wind up as an example of becoming more than what you thought, or ought to be. Be all you can be in the Army is not the result of individual effort. Instead it is due to the movements, motivation, and mentorship of many folks. It is the inertia and combined support of soldiers, families, friends, employers, and community. It is the synchronization of dual careers and family which allow reservists to be successful, such as Sergeant Fow, 98th Division Soldier of the Year; Sergeant First Class Lamm, NCO of the Year; Sergeant First Class Henderson, Drill Sergeant of the Year; Sergeant First Class Hasan, Retention NCO of the Year; and Master Sergeant Kuffrey, Instructor of the Year. It is my privilege to lead this esteemed division and soldiers like these. Thanks for having me in the 98th Division Family.

According to Martin Luther King, Jr., the true neighbor will risk his position, his prestige, and even his life for the welfare of others. In dangerous valleys and hazardous pathways, he will lift some bruised and beaten brother to a higher and more noble life. America is the true global neighbor. America's resolve resonates from the inaugural words of President Kennedy: "Let every nation know, whether it wishes us well or ill, that we shall pay any price, bear any burden, meet any hardship, support any friend, oppose any foe, in order to assure the survival and the success of liberty." Our soldiers stand point across the globe as true international neighbors. Let us pray that God will protect, strengthen, and sustain our servicemen and women who provide hope and comfort around the world to those who are suffering and afraid.

The "Army of One" is a body of one, like the natural or spiritual body. For our physical body is one, and hath many members. The foot is not the hand and the ear is not the eye, but they are of the body. And the eye cannot say unto the hand I have no need of thee: nor the head to the feet I have no need of thee. If the whole body were an eye, where were the hearing? If the whole were hearing where were the smelling? But they are many members but one body. The Army of One is one body and hath many contributing members, yet one body, one Army. The active component (AC) cannot say to the reserve component (RC) I have no need of you. If the whole Army were combat support, where is combat service support? And if all were maneuver, where is combat sustainment? The 98th Division is a body of one, and hath many members. Initial entry training (IET) cannot say to the Army School Sysytem (TASS) I have no need of you. If all were IET, where is TASS? If all were TASS, where is training support? The 98th division is a body of one; when one member is honored all are honored, and when one member suffers, all suffer. For two are better than one, for if one fall, one will lift up the other. Oneness does not dictate total agreement all the time. But at the conclusion of debate and discussion the body moves in unity for the common goal. Mission first, and soldiers always. Today the Army is challenged with transformation while at war. As we transform doctrine, formations, and equipment we must be prepared individually and collectively to meet the calls and challenges which lie ahead.

"HOOHAH" is an undefined term used in the Army. I believe it means I hear you, I agree, I'm trained, ready and motivated. If so, LET HOOHAH REIGN! Let HOOHAH reign from the rugged coast of Maine, the forest of Vermont, and the granite hills of New Hampshire. Let HOOHAH reign from the vineyards of Martha, the commons of Boston, and the ivy towers of New Haven and New London. Let HOOHAH reign from the prestigious waters of Rhode Island, Long Island, and the Jersey shore. Let HOOHAH reign from the monuments of Manhattan to the majestic mountains of the Empire State. Let HOOHAH reign from Dix, to Devens, to Drum, to West Point. Not only that, but let HOOHAH reign from every armory, reserve center, fort, base and installation. Let it reign from the barracks and homes in this region. If the 98th Division lets HOOHAH reign we will promptly fill our unit vacancies and expeditiously train our soldiers awaiting DMOSQ. We will improve readiness through innovative recruitment, aggressive retention, strict stewardship of resources, and proven relevance. If we let HOOHAH reign we will train the MPs of the 800th MP, the medics of the 8th MED, the engineers of the 411th, and the soldiers of the 353rd Civil Affairs. We will be an indispensable partner in the production of young warriors at Forts Leonard-Wood and Knox, and the grooming of warrior leaders in ROTC and the Military Academy. We will meet our customers' needs and become their trainers of choice.

98th Division, can we do this? Can we do this in the region that gave us JFK and Colin Powell? In the area that educated Martin Luther King, Jr., and Norman Schwarzkopf? In the birthplace of Reserve Officer Training, ROTC? In the area that houses 60% of the nation's service academies and 40% of our reserve installations?

YOU BET WE CAN AND WE SHALL!

The American Creed was adopted by the House of Representatives in 1918. The American Creed: "I believe in the United States of America as a government of the people, by the people, for the people: whose just powers are derived from the consent of the governed: a democracy in a republic: a sovereign nation of many sovereign states: a perfect union, one and inseparable: established upon the principals of freedom, equality, justice, and humanity for which American Patriots sacrificed their lives and fortunes. I therefore believe it is my duty to my country to love it, to support its constitution, to obey its laws, to respect its flag, and to defend it against enemies.

I am proud to be an American Soldier! In God We Trust! United We Stand!

My vision was to conduct business in a more dynamic fashion. This would, however, require a break with tradition. We needed newness, a paradigm shift. Because change had to start with senior leadership, I reshuffled commanders, command sergeant majors and the division staff. I selected Command Sergeant Major William (Bill) Grocott as the 98th Division Command Sergeant Major and we set out to meet our Iroquois Warrior Family. My first priority was to travel to every unit location and meet with as many soldiers and civilians as possible to articulate my vision and seek their buy-in. In addition we made sure that subordinate leaders understood their missions and encouraged them to strive for efficient productivity in the delivery of training to the Army.

We had to do things differently because the Army's need for the accelerated training of soldiers was increasing due to the Global War on Terrorism (GWOT). To me innovative business practices demanded that we make better use of the inactive and active duty days available to Reserve Soldiers. This meant the consolidation of inactive and active duty days to provide more classes. The response from my subordinates was somewhat mixed, but for the most part people supported breaking out of the weekend warrior mentality and exploring new options.

CHAPTER ELEVEN

INTERRUPTION OF EVERYTHING

I was returning from a trip and was walking through the Richmond Airport the late evening of March 20, 2003, when I saw the late evening news showing the invasion of Iraq by U.S. and Coalition forces, dubbed Operation Iraqi Freedom (OIF). Although I was aware that operational plans for the invasion had been in the works for several months I had a bad feeling about the military operations since Secretary of Defense Donald Rumsfeld had rebuffed the advice of the Army Chief of Staff, General Eric Shinseki, regarding the required troop strength.

On May 6th President George W. Bush declared that Operation Iraqi Freedom was a success and announced the cessation of major military operations in Iraq. In the meantime the Pentagon was abuzz with apprehension. Things had not progressed as the Secretary of Defense had predicted. Operation Iraqi Freedom became entangled in insurgency activity with unknown enemies. This would be unconventional warfare, which the United States was ill equipped to handle. The absence of an exit strategy, in contradiction of the "Powell Doctrine," which articulates that no military operation should be initiated without first having an exit strategy, complicated matters. Unconventional warfare is a prolonged fight often waged in urban setting among civilians, which is a soldier's worst nightmare. With two simultaneous wars in Iraq and Afghanistan the Army was in trouble trying to sustain the long wars. The continuous mobilization of the Army National Guard and Army Reserve was now reality. The Army Operations Center, buried in the deep bowels of the Pentagon, monitored world wide operations around the clock and searched for solutions to fill critical manpower requirements. The Army was struggling to sustain the long wars. Such would require multiple rotations of Army units, both active and reserve components. Because the Army Reserve houses the bulk of the Army's combat support elements – engineers, military police, signal, and chemical; and combat service support elements – civil affairs, personnel, logistics, transportation, and medical – it was indispensably involved in the war from the beginning. We were instructed to prepare for mobilization. President Bush had authorization to call up reservists in support of Operation Iraqi Freedom and Operation Enduring Freedom (Afghanistan).

There are two categories of soldiers in the Army Reserve: troop program soldiers (TPU), formerly dubbed "weekend warriors," who are assigned to units and engage in regular training; and individual ready reservists (IRR), who are usually a name on a roster to be pulled as the last resort. It was anticipated that large numbers if IRR soldiers would have to be mobilized to support the war effort. It was the mission of Institutional Training Divisions, such as the 98th Division, to retrain the lackluster IRR soldiers as they were ordered to active service. There was a huge problem in identifying and assessing the usability of IRR soldiers because there was an inadequate accounting system for them. It seemed that some had just vanished and most were not interested or available for duty because of medical problems, or employment and family issues. Ideally IRR soldiers would be mobilized, trained, and assigned to fill the personnel vacancies in existing units. There was very limited success using IRR soldiers, so the Army Reserve resorted to "cross leveling," or borrowing soldiers from one unit to fill up another unit. The end result was the rapid depletion of manpower and an inability to build other units capable of deployment.

Sergeant Lawrence Roukey was a postal worker and Iroquois Warrior from Maine. I remember Larry from my visits to his unit in Lewiston, Maine. Larry was my designated driver for the short trip from the Portland airport to Lewiston. He was an adventurous type and made the trips interesting as he zipped through traffic, and could have easily qualified as a New York cabbie. He had served on active duty in Korea and joined the Army Reserve following the September 11th attacks. Sergeant Roukey was ordered to active duty and was reassigned to an Army engineer unit in Iraq and served on the Iraqi Survey Team that searched for weapons of mass destruction. On April 26, 2004, he was killed while providing security outside a warehouse that was suspected of containing weapons. The warehouse exploded killing Larry Roukey. On a sunny May 7, 2004, Larry's Iroquois Warrior Family joined the Roukey Family and the entire town of Westbrook, Maine, the governor, a U.S. senator, a U.S. congressman, and other dignitaries to celebrate the life of Larry Roukey. School children lined the streets along the funeral procession to the cemetery holding small American flags to honor their local hero. Larry Roukey was thirty-three and was survived by his wife Ryann and two children. Larry's memory is preserved by a plaque in his honor displayed in the Portland, Maine, Post Office. A building bearing his name was dedicated in his honor at Fort Dix, New Jersey. Larry is at rest in the Calvary Cemetery, South Portland, Maine. Unfortunately this was the first of several funerals for fallen Iroquois Warriors. Four funerals were to follow.

Since flawed U.S. strategy virtually wiped out all authority in Iraq by disbanding the Iraqi Army and police forces, there was an absence of civil order there. Thus there was an urgent need to increase the size of the Iraqi Security Forces, consisting of the Iraqi Army and police forces.

The Army Reserve had given some consideration to the concept of providing training to foreign countries prior to Operation Iraqi Freedom. The Institutional Training Divisions had developed a concept plan for a Foreign Army Training and Assistance Command (FA-TRAC), but nothing more. We were, after all, training assets, and it was logical to have transportable training assets capable of operating anywhere. FA-TRAC was to be flexible and transportable to foreign soil. The 98th Division was assigned the task of creating a concept plan for an organization to be the Foreign Army Training and Assistance Command, Iraq (FA-TRAC-I). Then the questions and concerns began to roll in. Was a mission in a combat zone appropriate for the reserves? Why not use the Special Forces? Soldiers within the command asked, "Why us?" The Army was out of resources and the need for the Iraqi Security Forces to be rapidly expanded was a reality. There was little support for the concept outside of the Army Operation Center, which monitored worldwide operations and had run out of programmable resources. LTG James Helmly, Chief of the Army Reserve, gave his blessings to study the feasibility of the mission. Things then developed quickly. Within two months the concept plan was receiving serious consideration. Then the typical Army burearacracy kicked in and questioned everything. There was little support from the United States Army Forces Command, which has the mission of generating troop units from U.S.-based forces for the war fight. The Army Reserve Command to which we reported was not much help either.

LTG David Petraeus had commanded the 101st Airborne Division during the invasion of Iraq, and was selected to command the Multi-National Security Transition Command-Iraq (MNSTC-I). He came to Washington in June 2004 to brief Congress, and was in search of resources for the yet to be defined exit strategy. BG Richard Sherlock, Deputy Commander 98th Division, and I first met LTG Petraeus in a conference room in the Pentagon for an information briefing on Army Reserve Training assets. He was unfamiliar with the capabilities resident in the Army Reserve, and became interested when he learned about potential assets.

He wanted to know if we could get folks on the ground right away to make an assessment. He was unfamiliar with the antiquated mobilization process for activating Army Reserve soldiers.

Following that meeting we met with the Chief of the Army Reserve, LTG Helmly, for a decision brief. The Director of the Army Operations Center, Major General Douglas Robinson, presented his case for the urgency of the mission. LTG Helmly approved the use of Army Reserve assets for the mission, and plans were made for the near immediate departure of members of my Command Team to conduct as assesment. I turned to my Chief of Staff, Colonel Frank Cippola, and asked how soon he could be on the move. He said, "Sir, I'll call my employer and let them know I won't be back." Colonel Cippola and other soldiers reported to Fort Bliss, Texas, to be immediately processed for duty in Iraq. They were the advance party for the Survey Team that had the assignment of traveling throughout Iraq to make an assessment of what was needed for the mission of rapidly expanding and training the Iraqi security forces. The Survey Team headed by BG Sherlock was hand-picked from our most gifted officers and senior noncommissioned officers. They prepared to report to Fort Bliss, Texas, right after Independence Day.

Fortunately BG Sherlock had worked in the Pentagon and knew how to work around the Army and Pentagon bureaucracy. He was able to snag the right people to assist with conducting the survey. The Survey Team was like an architect trying to design something from a rudimentary sketch. A similar mission had already been started, but because it lacked definition and resources and was an uncoordinated effort, there was little to build from.

Army Reserve soldiers usually receive a mobilization alert so they can have maximum time to plan for their activation and mobilization. I assembled my senior leaders in mid June to inform them of the possible mission and issued an alert notification for the entire division, because we had no idea as to who we would need. We did know that we would need Training Assistance Teams who would live with and train the Iraqi forces. Normally drill sergeants would fill the bill. However, the criteria were mature male NCOs possessing good counseling skills and patience. This was going to be a cultural shift from the American way of training recruits. Therefore, in-your-face drill sergeants would not do. After projecting the numbers needed, commanders and their command sergeant majors took on the job of personally interviewing prospective candidates and recommending the right people.

Once the alert was published there were many surprises. There was the immediate defection of many senior people, colonels, lieutenant colonels, and master sergeants, who elected immediate retirement rather than risk being mobilized. Then there were the crybabies

– journalist, politicians, employers, family members, and soldiers questioning why the 98th Division had to be deployed to Iraq. Someone leaked sensitive information to the news media in an effort to create a public outcry against using the 98th Division for such a mission. It did not work. With our military and civilian skills we were capable of doing the mission, and there was no unit better qualified than us. In addition, we hailed from New England, New York, and New Jersey, and their neighboring states, and had more diversity and looked more like America than anyone else. What I didn't share was that, as a result of the transformation of the Army Reserve, the 98th Division had been earlier declared excess baggage and was slated to slim down to be the headquarters of the Foreign Army Training Command. We had actually written the script on the subject in prior years and apparently someone had actually read it. Now we were preparing to execute the script. We had no doubt about our ability to do the mission.

As we neared mobilization there were alibis, usually for family and employment hardships, which were handled on an individual basis. Most would just require an adjustment to the mobilization dates so as to handle a temporary personal situation. Overall our soldiers had great attitudes and were divided into several categories because of the need for rapid call-up. There were those volunteers willing to waive the required thirty-day mobilization notice and report immediately upon receipt of the official mobilization order; and those who would report as directed after receiving the required thirty-day notice. The special needs of the mission required bringing in soldiers with the requisite skills from throughout the Army Reserve. Most were drilling reservists and others were parked in the IRR. Some of the IRR soldiers had not worn a uniform for many years and came in kicking and screaming about their call-up. There was criticism from their relatives, questioning the wisdom of calling up couch potatoes, and politicians chimed in with Congressional inquires. In the end they were whipped into shape, trained, and deployed. They made a significant contribution to the mission of assisting in the building of the emerging Iraqi Security Forces.

The Division Command Sergeant Major, CSM Grocott, and I traveled extensively to sell the concept to our soldiers and families. The Division Operations Center was set up within the division headquarters and we prepared for what was to come. The Deputy Chief of Staff for Operations (G3), Colonel Bradford Parsons, headed the operation. Without much guidance we would have to figure it out as we went along. Colonel Parsons and BG Sherlock were the major architects of what would follow. We knew we were in for a bumpy ride. It was like building a plane already in flight.

The longer the wait between alert notification and mobilization, the more anxiety there is among soldiers and their families. Since the September 11th attacks, Army Reserve soldiers have been keenly aware of the real possibility of mobilization and have seriously prepared for that possibility, because the Army Reserve has been an operational force since that time. However, there was a huge gap in family readiness despite Family Readiness Programs and other efforts intended to educate and assist families to prepare for the mobilization of their soldiers.

BG Sherlock was called back to the U.S. to present his initial assessment to the U.S. Army Forces Command (FORSCOM) prior to the Army preparing a request for forces, justifying the need for troops. Such a request must then be validated before anything happens. BG Sherlock was coolly received by the Operations types at FORSCOM, who had little interest in providing the resources for the mission. Pressure from theater finally cut through the log jam. Finally we received the mobilization order shortly before Labor Day weekend. On the third anniversary of the September 11th attacks, Iroquois Warriors of the 98th Division (Institutional Training) began to mobilize from throughout our region. Soldiers departed by bus, train, car, and plane for their respective mobilization stations for processing and training.

Those going to staff positions at MNSTC-I headed for Fort Bliss, Texas. Those going to be military advisors departed for Camp Atterbury, Indiana. I sent Colonel Robert Catalanotti, the 1st Brigade Commander, to head operations at Camp Atterbury. Once Army Reserve soldiers are mobilized they are no longer assigned to their parent organization. Instead they fall under the control of the First U.S. Army for processing and training. At Camp Atterbury the training required for Iraq was inadequately defined. The result was wasted time on unnecessary training, such as land navigation in wooded areas. Our soldiers at Fort Bliss were needed first because they were staff and needed to get things in place. They therefore received abbreviated training at Fort Bliss, to be followed up in Kuwait and Iraq. CSM Grocott and I spent considerable time at both sites mingling with our soldiers. We were there as the planes lifted off for Kuwait from Fort Bliss and Indianapolis. As our soldiers were being trained and deployed we had a war to sell to families, so we conducted town hall meetings. My promise to our soldiers was that if they deployed we would look out for their families and protect their interests back home.

On December 21, 2004, CNN continually ran the story of a dining tent suicide bombing in Iraq. The news spread rapidly that an Iroquois Warrior was among the casualties. Master Sergeant Paul Karpowich was an advisor to the new Iraqi Army. He had served on active duty with the 82nd Airborne Division. I remember Paul from visits to his unit in Pennsauken, New

Jersey, and to Camp Atterbury. His big smile and generous heart were unforgettable. He was all soldier and inspired others to excel. "No bellyaching, No sniveling, No excuses, Suck it Up" was his mantra as he demanded one more push-up and another sit-up from soldiers. Paul had finished his lunch but stayed back in the mess tent at Forward Operating Base Marez in Mozel to advise an Iraqi Army officer, when the explosion took their lives along with twenty others. On a fridgid December 31, 2004, Iroquois Warriors joined the Karpowich Family and the community of Freeland, Pennsylvania, to celebrate the life of Paul Karpowich. As the horse-drawn funeral wagon carrying Paul traveled through the streets followed by a military formation the entire town filled the sidewalks to honor their fallen hero. Paul was thirty years old and was survived by his wife Amanda. Paul is at rest in the Arlington National Cemetery.

As the vision for the design of the Iraqi Army took shape there were requests for more soldiers as the need for training Iraqi logisticians, transporters, mechanics and medical personnel was recognized. The end result was the exhaustion of my senior leadership. We anted up most of my colonels which left CSM Grocott and me with skeletal leadership. Owing to the fast pace at which events were happening, many families were ill-informed of what was taking place and why. We therefore embarked on a series of town hall meetings throughout the Northeast and Paducah, Kentucky, for the purpose of educating our families, employers, and the community. In addition we built a robust family support network, with local representatives tied together electronically.

We opened each town hall meeting with one of our deployed soldiers calling in to provide an overview of the situation in Iraq. We then fielded questions and assisted with problems. Personnel, finance, and legal assistance teams were present during the meetings to help family members with problems. Through my open door policy I learned of problems and moved to quickly resolve them. Mobilization orders were a big issue. The problem was with the Office of the Secretary of Defense (OSD), which had to approve every mobilization order. That only happened once a week, to the frustration of the Army Staff. Because there was a cap on the number of Reservists who could be mobilized, other categories for bringing soldiers on active duty were used that did not count against the cap. In effect there were disguised means to keep the numbers down so as not to rile Congress or the public. So if a soldier was needed immediately, he was called to duty under some other category. The end result was extended duty for some, because the other categories of active duty did not count against the 12-month, then 15-month mobilization period for Reservists.

Of particular concern during the meetings was the disparity between living conditions and facilities at the various duty stations for our soldiers. Unlike most reserve units, which stay together, our soldiers were disbursed throughout the country, in varying conditions because we were just getting the training bases established. Some had access to the Internet and phones, but most did not. Some soldiers were bored, while others were busy. Soldiers understood, but some family members did not. One of the problems of modern-day warfare is operational security, due to America's insatiable appetite for instantaneous information. The Internet and cell phones make controlling the flow of information difficult. The mishandling of information such as a casualty can be devastating.

Personnel turbulence was inevitable. I reserved the final decision on all personnel issues. My Blackberry and cell phone were ever present, and the Assistant Division Personnel Officer making the assignments and I talked often. Major John Vernick masterfully handled the filling of vacancies that required a soldier of a particular rank and military specialty. These were last-minute call-ups that gave the affected soldiers little time to report because they had to receive mandatory training and meet a deployment schedule. Sometimes there was as little as 24-hour notice, which was contrary to Army policy, but dictated by need.

Loyalty drives soldiers to answer the call to duty with little hesitation despite personal and professional hardship. Here are a few examples: One of the members of the Survey Team, a single parent, left his dying mother and two sons on short notice to fulfill the needs of the Army. Another soldier, borrowed from another reserve unit, was given twenty-four-hour notice to report. His chain of command contacted me with various reasons why he should not be deployed; the major concern being complications with his wife's pregnancy. We were able to negotiate a seventy-two-hour reporting time after our Family Support Group rushed to his aid and made arrangements to assist his wife during his absence. He returned home to a healthy newborn child. We received twelve soldiers from the 100th Division (Institutional Training) from a unit in Paducah, Kentucky, dubbed the "Paducah Dozen." They trained at Camp Atterbury, Indiana, and were granted passes right before departing for Iraq. One soldier's pregnant wife was due to deliver their child during his leave period, but the child refused to cooperate as they waited in the hospital. So the sergeant rushed back by the appointed time. While waiting at the Indianapolis Airport to board his plane his cell phone signaled that his son had arrived. An airline staff member was able to get the picture he received of his child over his cell phone printed in time for boarding. He held his son for the first time when he returned home for his mid-tour leave six months later.

CSM Grocott and I spent as much time as we could with our soldiers before they departed, to thank them and their families for their service. I learned that there were a number of mothers and fathers leaving their young children entrusted to others. I learned that many risked the loss of income and possibly jobs as a result of being deployed. I learned that there was a large number of self employed soldiers, accountants, contractors, farmers, lawyers, shop owners, who walked away from their livelihoods with the confidence and faith that upon their return they could restart them. Their attitude was, "I have a mission to perform and I'll deal with that when I return." Part of being a Reserve soldier is planning for what-ifs. I too had a mobilization business plan for my office which I did not have to execute because the Army elected not to mobilize CSM Grocott or me because of other missions the 98th Division was assigned to perform. Instead BG Sherlock would head up the FA-TRAC-I mission. My law office arrangements were for my office manager to handle what work was already in progress, and to refer all other work out to a series of attorneys who agreed to take it on. Then when I returned I would assess my office situation and adjust accordingly.

In addition to the FA-TRAC mission, the 98th Division still had other training missions to perform, including training new soldiers at Fort Leonard Wood, Missouri, and other training posts. I needed help from some of my senior leaders who were in Iraq and was able to trade some colonels. I was able to get Colonel William Clegg, Assistant Division Commander (ADC), Colonel Frank Cippola, Chief of Staff (C/S), and Colonel Paul Womack, Division Chaplain back to help me. Colonel Catalanotti, who headed the Camp Atterbury operation and knew each soldier personally, went to Iraq to command the Taji Training Base. Colonel Michael Smith, C/S and ADC, went to Iraq to assist with police training. The Iraq returnees were able to add more credibility and accurate information to our town hall meetings. My most memorable event was on the tiny island of Isleboro, Maine. The island had full-time inhabitants and some celebrity property owners. We barely made it to the ferry in time for boarding. Isleboro is a small picturesque island, and we were warned that the last return trip was at a particular time. The driver of the small school bus that picked us up at the pier was also the local tour guide, historian, and gossiper. The lone schoolhouse instructed all grades, kindergarten through twelfth. The entire island came out for the barbecue chicken dinner held in honor of one of its own soldiers. The community was a haven for retirees, some of whom were from as far away as Georgia. The local band of seniors provided the music as a young singer belted out the National Anthem and other songs. As we ate and mingled with the crowd I took little notice of the time until someone mentioned that if we got stranded they could always pull out cots and blankets in the gymnasium. We missed the last ferry but caught a ride on the water taxi, which also served as the mail carrier's transportation.

Staff Sergeant Christopher Dill was a firefighter from Buffalo, New York. He had served on active duty with the 24th Infantry Division during the Gulf War. He was part of the Advisory Support Team assigned to the 6th Battalion, 5th Division, of the new Iraqi Army. The team helped train Iraqi soldiers. On April 4, 2005, a bullet took the life of Christopher Dill as he was engaged in combat against insurgents in Balad Ruz, Iraq. The Iroquois Warrior family joined a large gathering in Tonawanda, New York, on April 15, 2005, to celebrate the life of Christopher Dill. Two fire ladder trucks with fully extended ladders formed an arch displaying a huge American flag. Chris was thirty-two and was survived by his wife Dawn. The Vertical Skills Building at Fort Dix, New Jersey, was dedicated to the Memory of Christopher W. Dill on June 11, 2005. Chris is at rest in the Mt. Olivet Cemetery, Tonawanda, New York.

CSM Grocott and I traveled to Iraq in mid-April 2005 to visit our soldiers. We flew from Atlanta to Frankfurt, Germany, thence to Kuwait City by commercial airline. We were picked up by our escort officer and whisked off in an SUV to the military base. In Kuwait we received operational briefs and got the official tour before we boarded an Air Force C-130 for the ride to Iraq. We visited our troops at Camp Victory and in the "Green Zone," Baghdad's fortified area. From there we climbed aboard Blackhawk helicopters to visit our soldiers who were deployed in forward training bases. We were able to convey our appreciation to our soldiers and address their concerns. During our visit to the Balad Ruz area we found our Iroquois Warriors still tense from the recent combat that claimed the life of Chris Dill. We also met with the senior leadership of the emerging Iraqi Army and police force. Personal relationships are essential to getting things done in Iraq, and having the right people in place was critical to the success of missions. A tremendous bonding process took place between our soldiers and the Iraqis. Iraq is a country of vast contrasts in its geography, resources, culture, and standards of living. As we flew from place to place the conspicuous absence of an organized government was evident. Governmental functions like sanitation were absent and trash was everywhere. Sanitation and personal hygiene had to be taught to most new Iraqi recruits. Thus our anticipated year-long deployment was reduced to a week's visit.

Lieutenant Colonel Terrence Crowe was an educator from Grand Island, New York. He had served on active duty with the 2nd Armored Division in Garlstedt, Germany. He was an advisor to an Iraqi unit. I remember Terry from Camp Atterbury, where he presented as a very serious leader and championed his fellow soldiers to stay focused on their training. On June 7, 2005, we were notified that LTC Crowe was killed while on patrol when his unit came under intense enemy attack. His Iroquois Warrior family joined the Crowe Family and the community of Grand Island, New York on a rainy June 16, 2005, to celebrate the life of Terrence Crowe. Terry arrived at the Buffalo Airport in the midst of a rain storm and the New York State Police volunteered to escort him home. He was survived by two children. An athletic field was dedicated on Grand Island in his honor. A building in his honor was dedicated at Fort Dix, New Jersey. He is at rest in Saint Stephen's Cemetery, Grand Island, New York.

Sergeant First Class Robert Derenda was from Cheektowaga, New York, and had served on active duty in Korea and Panama. He was a second-time Iroquois Warrior. He had served in the 98th Division before relocating to Kentucky and joining the 100th Division. He convinced his fellow soldiers from his unit in Paducah, Kentucky, to join him for the FA-TRAC mission. The twelve soldiers were dubbed the "Paducah Dozen." The Paducah Dozen were recognizable as a tight band of Kentucky brethren. They were together at the Indianapolis Airport waiting for their departure flight to Kuwait when news arrived that SSG Baker's son was finally born. They snapped a departure photo before boarding their plane. CSM Grocott and I saluted our soldiers as their plane taxied for departure.

On August 5, 2005, SFC Derenda was in a Humvee when the swerve of a civilian fuel truck claimed his life and the life of a fellow soldier. The Iroquois Warrior Family and Century (100th Division) Family joined the Derenda Family and the Buffalo, New York, community to celebrate the life of Bob Derenda on August 13, 2005. I met his parents, Valven and Loretta Derenda, at the funeral home. They had emigrated from Poland. As I was greeting members of the Derenda family from as far away as the Midwest I heard an unfamiliar language and was told it was Polish. I was asked to say a few words at Robert's funeral mass, so I took a crash course in Polish.

I nervously rose for my remarks during the mass and began with, "Dzien dobry rodzinie i gosciom" (good morning, family and friends). I then shared a few remarks about Bob's adventures in the Army Reserve that I had gathered from his buddies. Afterward at the family reception I got a lot of hugs and greetings in Polish and was dubbed the Polish General by mom and pop Derenda. On August 18, 2005, we reassembled at Arlington National Cemetery, where Robert Derenda was laid to rest. It was my first experience with an interment at Arlington. This is a special place, and it is moving to witness the special care and honor given to a Fallen American Soldier. A building in honor of Robert Derenda was dedicated at Fort Dix, New Jersey, on February 23, 2007. Members of the Paducah Dozen were there for the ceremony.

Our soldiers began to redeploy from Iraq in the fall of 2005. Prior to their deployment I had expressed the desire to have a formal history of our experiences with contributions from all sources wanting to contribute to the project. A small staff was created to put together a simple publication. The final product was a magnificent book entitled: "An Encounter with History, the 98th Division and the Global War on Terrorism, 2001-2005." It offers a better understanding of our contributions to Iraq and other countries. Our soldiers, who performed so magnificently, each received a copy of the book. The Army Reserve recognizes its soldiers with a nice Welcome Home Warrior package, including a flag shadow box, special USAR flag, lapel pins, and a special coin. We added a Certificate of Appreciation for each family and a special 98th Division GWOT (Global War on Terrorism) coin, which was designed by one of the deploying soldiers as we ate together at Camp Atterbury.

The 98th Division Command Group traveled to Fort Bliss, Camp Atterbury, and various locations in New England, New York, New Jersey, Kentucky, and Georgia to conduct the Welcome Home Warrior ceremonies. These were wonderful opportunities to recognize our soldiers before their families, employers, and communities. The berth of the Iroquois Warrior Family was extended to include hundreds of Soldiers assembled from 22 states and 44 Army Reserve units.

On the fourth anniversary of the September 11th attacks and the start of the Global War on Terrorism the Army Reserve and the Town on Freeland reassembled to dedicate a monument to "Fallen Heroes of The War on Terrorism from the Freeland Area." Paul Karpowich is the first name inscribed on the monument. A building named in honor of Paul Karpowich was dedicated at Fort Dix, New Jersey, on July 29, 2006. Starting with the inaugural event in the fall of 2005 at Valley Forge National Park, every fall in Southeastern Pennsylvania the Paul Karpowich Foundation sponsors the Paul Karpowich Memorial March, consisting of a 5- and 10-mile course in honor of Paul Karpowich and to raise funds for his legacy of giving to others. I arrived early for the march on the beautiful morning of October 16, 2008, to an energy-filled park, with Paul's wife Amanda and mother Jackie encouraging the volunteers and attendees. I noted much exuberance over the event, as a crowd of girls registered for the march. They were a soccer team, sent over by their coach. Some of their mothers asked about the meaning of the march. I led them to the table of mementoes honoring Paul Karpowich. I told them his story and explained that he was an American Soldier and this was his legacy, and that although Paul was not with us physically he is ever present with us in spirit.

My final journey with the Army Reserve first took me to Carlisle, Pennsylvania, for the Army War College graduation on July 27, 2007. I was there with my command team, consisting of Colonel Robert Catalanotti, ADC and Division Command Sergeant Major, CSM Milton Newsome. At the graduation a distinguished-looking gentleman told me that he had been my Tactical Officer at West Point. He was Colonel (Retired) Terry Wallace. He had been my company's second tac officer. He related to me that he had observed me as a cadet and had seen much potential in me. It's a small army world. CSM Newsome drove us to Rochester right after the graduation. From there we headed by commercial airline to Fort Jackson, South Carolina, to attend my final Drill Sergeant School graduation as division commander on July

28th. As I recognized my final crop of drill sergeants with a special coin, I noted that many of them were combat veterans. The Army Reserve had come full circle. We were real soldiers too.

After graduation we rushed back to Rochester by military aircraft, which was a rarity. It was a Navy UC 128 aircraft operating out of Naval Reserve Air Station Willow Grove, Pennsylvania, just outside of Philadelphia. I peered out of the window of the propeller-driven airplane, thinking about my long, unanticipated military journey, taking me from Pennsylvania to places around the globe. Now on the final leg of my journey I was being chauffeured by folks from Willow Grove, one of the communities where my day work experience had begun. I had come full circle. I had realized the American Dream.

We arrived back in Rochester just in time for a wonderful retirement bash at the division headquarters, thrown by my Iroquois Warrior Family that night. Under a brilliant sun on Sunday, July 29, 2007, I passed the colors of the 98th Division (Institutional Training) to its new commander Colonel (Promotable) Robert Catalanotti, and my two star general officer flag was rolled up and cased. Thus I retired from the United States Army. In attendance were numerous family members and a host of friends. My Mom was there from the start on July 1, 1966, to the finish on July 29, 2007. And in attendance were my sister and brothers David and Clarence, as well as numerous uncles, aunts and cousins. My West Point classmate Willie Price, who now lives in Minnesota, and law school classmate Brenda Friend Briggs also graced me with their presence. I received special recognition from the City of Rochester and Monroe County.

As I looked over my final formation of Iroquois Warriors I pondered what we had done. We had definitely made an impact. We had sent soldiers forward in harm's way to support the Global War on Terrorism. We were true global neighbors in Iraq, Afghanistan, Kuwait, Horn of Africa, Bosnia, and numerous other neighborhoods around the world. We led transformation in the Army Reserve by demonstrating expeditionary force capabilities. We molded leaders, and made NCOs and officers. We grew drill sergeants and instructors who collectively trained multitudes of American soldiers and brought hope to people of foreign lands. Our women had led men in combat and our young warriors had inspired us all. We were a Family of One. When one member was honored, we all were honored, and when one member suffered we all suffered. We endured triumph and tragedy; illness and recovery; births and deaths. We laughed together and cried together. We mourned the loss of our brothers: Larry, Paul, Chris, Terry, and Bob together. This was a day of honor for the Iroquois Family of One. I cried during my final remaks.

My grandsons had helped me clear my office and pack up my belongings earlier in the month. My Iroquois Warrior Family was gracious with gifts and tokens of appreciation. Everything was loaded in my van and I eased out of Rochester on a beautiful August 1st and headed south on U.S. Highway 15. The mountain vistas and meandering rivers and streams provided a spectacular backdrop for my journey as I reflected on a beautiful America , whose amber waves of grain, and purple mountain majesties above her fruited plain I had witnessed from sea to shining sea. I had been blessed to have traveled from the Atlantic to the Pacific and beyond, and to have partaken of the wonderful bounty of endless American opportunity. The journey was somewhat reminiscent of my departure from West Point 37 years earlier with all my worldly possessions in the back of my new 1970 Dodge Challenger. Then I was off to a new start. Life was simpler back then when I left the secure cocoon of the U.S. Military Academy. This time I had grown up, having witnessed monumental changes around the globe that had actually put this nation more at risk now that terrorism was the new tactic of choice for our adversaries.

Of particular concern to me is the explosive use of the reserve component, which has been transformed from a strategic reserve to an operational force in constant use. With long wars our national memory fades and soldiers are soon forgotten or ignored. For the reserve components to survive the Army will have to do a better job in protecting our soldiers' jobs, as employers are signaling less patience with extended military duty. And America must do a better job of taking care of her veterans, especially those who are scarred, physically and mentally. Many war veterans will have to deal with post-traumatic stress disorder (PTSD). I recognized the devastating effect of war on my returning soldiers and established a wellness cell in the 98th Division for the purpose of monitoring and assisting combat veterans.

I pray that every soldier, sailor, marine, airman, coastguardsman and civilian affected by any war or tour of service will seek help early and stick with it. PTSD has no time limitation. I challenge every family and community to assist in this regard.

Having achieved the rank of major general and commanding at the general officer level was an achievement that I never envisioned. It has been an honor and privilege to have joined with many soldiers to serve the people of the United States of America. I closed my military career on August 1, 2007, after forty years in uniform from age seventeen through fifty-seven. The Army had taken mighty good care of me for a long time, for which I attempted to reciprocate. I appreciate the opportunities afforded me in and out of uniform. As far as I am concerned the United States Army is the world's premier institution for the development of a person's potential. The Army has not treated everyone right throughout its distinguished history, but during my generation it has done a phenomenal job. Today's Army is people-centered, and much energy is devoted to the development of individuals, admittedly for the sake of the Army. But the overall positive benefits to its soldiers are undeniable. Many of my colleagues started out in the Army with a high school diploma or GED and retired with master's degrees, PhDs, and professional degrees.

I wonder if every American understands what is required of her military servant; her Soldiers, Sailors, Marines, Airmen, and Coasties? And do we really comprehend what they must sacrifice? My Memorial Days are personal now and I will perpetually remember, honor, and memorialize fallen heroes like my five Iroquois Warrior Brothers: Larry Roukey, Paul Karpowich, Chris Dill, Terry Crowe, and Bob Derenda, who gave their all for the sake of others. No one has greater love than this, that someone would lay down his life for his friends.

It was not my intention to soldier so long, but soldiering is truly an affair of the heart.

PART V: REFLECTIONS

CHAPTER TWELVE

SPENDING TIME WITH SELF

I had always been surrounded by people since birth until retiring from the Army in 2007. I returned home to an empty nest. Before becoming an empty nester I was able to realize my fantastic American journey because of two strong ladies who chose to share part of their lives with me.

"Before a successful man there may be a good woman (pulling)."

Jannie (Jean) Wells was working near West Point, New York, when I met her. Despite her dislike of cadets I did manage to invade her space. Jean was from rural western Alabama, the little town of Reform. We adventurously cruised the hills of the Hudson Valley in my new Dodge Challenger. One time she pointed to what appeared to be a castle on the other side of the river. I told her I would take her there. We didn't find the castle but did find enough in each other to foster a fairy tale relationship and get married on her nineteenth birthday. Our family included our son Thomas Christopher (Chris) Robinson, and we lived in Georgia, Germany, New Jersey, Virginia, and Maryland.

We spent our developmental years growing up together. We matured together and we grew spiritually together. There wasn't a lot that we could ever agree on and spent a lot of energy in verbal combat. We both held high ambitions and supported each other's visions. We achieved our goals. I have a J.D., and she has a PhD. Jean is fiercely independent, a risk taker and willing to work long and hard for the things she wants. We traveled on three continents and saw a lot of the world together. We shared 17 marital years together and are friends.

"Beside a successful man there may be a good woman (walking)."

Daisy was an Army Reserve soldier when I met her. Despite her dislike for officers, she did allow me to invade her space. Daisy is from Mecklenburg County, Virginia. She had been married and had three children before joining the Army at age thirty-one, completing basic training, boot camp, at Fort Jackson, outrunning teenagers up Tank Hill and all, at age thirty-two. We were outdoors types, enjoying walking, running, biking, camping, and working the soil. We liked traveling, mountain hikes and strolling along the beach. Our family included three daughters, Tracey, Kimberly, and Natalie, before the addition of three grandchildren. We lived in South Hill.

Daisy and I had our disagreements, but we did build a custom built home together. She retired from the Army Reserve after serving twenty-one years and from her job after thirty years. We spent our upward mobility years together and traveled extensively throughout the United States. Although a soldier herself, she was frequently unable to comprehend or tolerate the tremendous demand the Army places on senior leaders. We have an investment of 17 years of marriage and are friends.

For the first time in five years I was able to look forward to spending considerable time at home. It was finally time to enjoy the custom-built home that took us two years to construct using self help. There would be no rules, no restrictions, and no debates. Maybe everyone should spend time with himself. In our busy world we seldom get to be alone with ourselves in private and really reflect upon important things. I discovered that there are disadvantages (cons) and advantages (pros) with living alone.

Top Ten Cons:
1. Lack of sharing blessings
2. Absence of endless laughter
3. Loss of navigator or right seat driver
4. Solitary witness of pretty sunrises
5. Solitary witness of colorful sunsets
6. Dulling of culinary skills
7. Stagnant wardrobe
8. No free advice
9. No health tips
10. Hazmatic condition of refrigerator

Top Ten Pros:
1. No toilet seat protocol
2. Can stay in underwear all day
3. No dietary rules
4. Everything is always in place
5. Wardrobe selections are correct
6. Command of remote control
7. Watching senseless funny movies
8. Conversations aren't English lessons
9. Hats are authorized anywhere
10. No DMZ (designated movement zone) in bed

Since retiring from the Army I have returned to the law business and have assumed a less hectic pace; wearing four hats: defense attorney, bankruptcy trustee, substitute judge and special justice. In addition I am still the senior member of the Board of Directors for the Virginia Legal Aid Society. I hope to get to the retirement thing in a few years and devote more time to volunteer work like with the Habitat for Humanity. These are the best of times for me. God has blessed me spiritually, physically, and financially. It has been an interesting and remarkable American journey under the guidance of Jesus Christ.

My days start out the same, with meditation and exercise. I intend to keep a healthy body and mind by monitoring my health, eating right, exercising, and alleviating stress. I take an annual physical. I have even lost a few pounds due to a consistent diet, exercise, good nutrition, and adequate rest. Because I prepare my meals at home and seldom eat out, I have a better idea of what is going into my body. I have even taken up long-distance running, participating in ten-milers and half marathons. I even participated in the Richmond Marathon in 2007, following the example of Paul Womack, my former division Chaplain, who completed a marathon in 2006 when he was age sixty something. I did three half marathon in 2008 in preparation for the 31st Richmond Marathon, which I intend to be my last full marathon.

Throughout my life there has always been the soft still voice of God calling me to trust him and obey his word. I was blessed with a sound mind and body. Preparation, patience, and perseverance, along with sacrifice and satisfaction will carry us a long way in life. Delaying present-day satisfaction for future gain enhances opportunity. Postponing material acquisition and sexual gratification for school and other opportunities pays big dividends in the long run.

There is nothing unique about success in America. The time honored formula of hard work, patience, dedication, and honesty usually works. Add to that a good attitude and aptitude for learning new things and you have a winning formula. Most American families as compared to the rest of the world are doing reasonably well in taking care of their basic needs. I emphasize the family, that core unit of society. It takes family work, like teamwork, for people to succeed. Every member has a part to play and every part is important for the overall success of a family. Throughout time the family is the core of all societies. Food, water, shelter, clothing, and security are essential human needs everywhere. The maintenance of a household is a communal effort, requiring all parties to make a contribution. In America we devote the majority of our free time to travel, leisure, and recreation. We spend a smaller percentage of our income for essential needs than most societies. As economic conditions change we must adjust to the reality that things are no longer the way they were, with the United States forcing its will on the rest of the world. We must now compete with other countries for resources, and when there is more demand there are more costs. However, such will not fundamentally affect the achievement of the American Dream. The dream may have to be adjusted, with smaller homes, plainer cars, and less leisure time. Throughout this country college and vocational education are reasonably accessible and affordable. Education costs because it is an investment. And if you think education is expensive, compare it to the cost of ignorance.

My generation, the Baby Boomers, has been reluctant to allow their offspring to handle adversity on their own. There must be standards and limits set, and the enforcement of them is essential. The constant shielding of individuals from suffering the consequences of their decisions robs them of the opportunity to achieve self sufficiency. I wonder if we try to do too much too soon with our limited resources. There is a constant enticement to buy newer and fancier stuff. Parents, wanting their children to have a better life than they had, refuse to allow their children to experience hardship or failure, which is a huge mistake. Failing is part of learning from mistakes, as falling down is part of learning to walk. To increase earnings we work longer hours, travel greater distance, and work more jobs. We fail to assess the limitations of finite resources as we overuse credit opportunities. We can do more with existing resources but choose not to do so for the sake of convenience or excitement. We could prepare more meals at home, drive cheaper cars, and live in plainer homes, but choose not to do so. When our children attempt to prematurely duplicate our lifestyles and fail, we rush to their aid. It is commendable to want to bail a child out of trouble, but such should not be done at one's own peril.

If you have good reason to help someone, I recommend the following:
1. Establish limits and adhere to them.
2. Provide assistance only once. Help with one car note, one house payment, one student loan payment, one pregnancy.
3. Don't lend what you can't afford to lose.

CHAPTER THIRTEEN

DEMONSTRATIVE LESSONS

It was the week preceding the Richmond Marathon that I sequestered myself in a quiet place in an effort to finish this book. I had worked late into the night and into the early morning. I still rose early and meditated on God's word before heading out for a long run on the trail along the river. Running along the water serves as an elixir and makes running a dozen miles more tolerable. Something strange came over me as I was enjoying nature coming alive in the early morning, with water cascading over the rocks, the birds singing, and the ducks swimming. As I was meditating on the goodness of God and witnessing how he takes care of all his creation, the birds in the field and all, I began to cry. I didn't know why. I was glad I was on the trail alone as tears rolled down my face. Fortunately no other soul was up that early as this supposedly tough guy was boo-hooing while negotiating the river trail. What was happening? I was receiving a revelation of God's Mercy and Grace from my heavenly Father as he revealed to me how he used my natural father and mother as his vessels to reveal himself to me and others; and how his goodness was manifested in and through my parents. They were in fact vessels used by him to reveal himself to others including me. Indeed I was truly Blessed. I wondered what would have happened differently if Dad had not been around. I pictured my mother as a widow with five small children to raise in the projects alone. I wondered if perhaps this story would have been different. I was assured that the answer was definitely not, because God takes care of his own. Then I witnessed the sun coming up in its full glory. This experience and the Richmond marathon helped me to close out this book.

I. Demonstrative Lessons from Dad

1. **Fight for your life.** Dad was severely injured in an industrial accident. I am told he died three times on the operating table but refused to stay dead, and his surgeon refused to give up. I believe Dad came back from the dead the first time for his wife, because he saw her burden. I think he came back the second time for his children. He came back for Eleanor, David, Clarence, Wayne, and ME. I think he came back the third time to be a witness for the love and mercy of GOD.

2. **Live with pain.** Dad was pieced together with screws and pins in his arm, leg, and hip, which occasionally bothered him. He would sit quietly meditating and tapping his good foot and endure the discomfort until it subsided.

3. **Take care of your family.** Dad was a product of a young mother, the Great Depression, and a large family. He willed himself well enough to return to work. He devised ways to live within his resources. He knew how to hustle, stretch food, hunt for bargains and do what was necessary to take care of his family. That is what fathers do.

4. **Be a servant.** Dad was always helping people. His station wagons would haul people and things and it seldom rested.

5. **Work as a family.** Do things as a family unit, from attending church, visiting, and grocery shopping, to doing chores.

II.   Demonstrative Lessons from Mom

1. **Provide for your family.** Mom was faithful in taking care of her broken husband and five children. For two years at times there was only $19.00 a week to cover all expenses – rent, food, and all else. She was creative in stretching whatever she had. Now she helps her kinfolks to a fault. She has taken care of her children, grandchildren, and great-grandchildren. She says, they are family, so if she has anything she will share it.

2. **Keep a roof over your head.** You have to have a place to live. Buy a house and make payments on time. You can find loose change for a loaf of bread. Someone may give you a piece of bread, but they can't put you up.

3. **Use money wisely.** Make do with what you have. Pay for housing, utilities, and food in that order. Use cash or money orders if you can't balance a checkbook. When you are out of money, you're just out of money.

4. **Be strong.** Strength comes when you need it. "Dad's foot slipped under the car when he fell on the ice on the way to his kidney dialysis treatment. I tried everything I could to get his foot out. Then I said, Dave, you'll have to pull your foot out when I lift the car. I don't know how I did it but I picked the car up enough for him to get his foot out."

5. **Be a caregiver.** When I came to Philadelphia I took care of my uncle who had a kidney operation. Then I took care of Dad for twenty-three years. I did what I could for Mother until Alzheimer's set in and she got to be too much for me. After my brothers took her back to Virginia they saw that with an Alzheimer's patient you need help.

III. Demonstrative Lessons from Our Heavenly Father

I signed up for the 31st Richmond Marathon against sound advice. My goal was to beat my time from the previous year's marathon. I was serious about beating my best time and trained accordingly. I even completed three half marathons in Virginia Beach, Philadelphia, and Richmond in hot, cool, and rainy weather in preparation for the event. I was disciplined with my seven-, ten-, thirteen-, and twenty-mile runs. My strategy was to run the first twenty miles with a walk/run during the last six miles. The previous year I started walking at mile seventeen, based on the signals from my body. Not this year. I was going to be in control and was determined to make it to mile twenty before walking. Actually I was psyched for 26 miles of continuous running. After all, a marathon is a race against yourself, your mental self, not those competing with you.

Marathons are community events, a big party of sorts, with people lining up along the entire route to cheer you on. The streets are filled with volunteers and residents offering their encouragement, and most runners have their personal cheering squads to motivate them. In addition there are high school cheerleaders offering encouragement, and bands playing along the route. You hear music like "The Impossible Dream" and know you can do it. You will get to the finish line.

By race time the early morning rain tapered off as the temperatures climbed into the 60s under a cloudy sky, with high winds which gave the runners some concern. As approximately 4,400 runners stirred with great anticipation in their corrals behind the starting line we were reminded to hydrate, to drink lots of fluids along the course. Each marathoner determines his own pace and tries to monitor himself by the official time clock at the mile markers. Some would run too fast at the beginning, and fade. Others would be injured along the way and not make it. But everyone is affected by the euphoria of the cheering crowds, the music, and their fellow runners, and wants to make it to the finish line. Finishing is the ultimate goal, and more important than a fast run. Some will come up from behind and pass you and you will pass others along the way, but you have to guard against the tendency of keeping pace with the people up front. It is your individual pace that is important, and no one else's.

As I reflected on the parallel between life's journey and the marathon I realized that I was called to run my final marathon for a reason. God wanted to teach me something that might otherwise be missed in my normal rushed life. He needed me to be quiet and attentive and there was no better place than during a four- or five-hour marathon. I began to take notice as I ran.

I crossed the starting line feeling pretty good. I had prepared well and my only concern was keeping my feet dry because of the rain. Things went well as we traversed some of Richmond's finest neighborhoods on the north side of town. Then we climbed a long hill and crossed the Huguenot Bridge, which took us to Southside Richmond with its array of fine homes along the James River in the Stratford Hills section of town. I knew the stretch pretty well because it was my old route to law school and I once lived nearby and enjoyed running along the river. The sun began to peak out when I was at the ten-mile point and feeling good. My time was on target. The James River with its gentle flow was an elixir and nature was coming alive in its full array of glory. For some unexplained reason everyone seemed to be energized and picked up speed along this stretch. I felt an unusual spirit around me, an unusual presence of peace and joy, and began to tear up. I wasn't hurting or anything, so why did I want to cry? My spirit told me to pay attention.

1. **God takes care of his children.**

God reminded me of the many times he had taken care of me despite my disobedience. I reflected back to December 10, 2000, when I was on Interstate 85 returning home from working on investment property. I had pinned on my brigadier general stars a week before and had celebrated the occasion in Richmond and at home, showing off our new home. I was at the top of my game but ignored the warning signs to slow down. So, late at night on a lonely, dark highway God gave me my final choice. I felt discomfort in my chest, a throbbing headache, weak and lousy all over. I thought it was from the paint and chemicals I had been using or indigestion from the pinto beans I had eaten. So I popped an aspirin under my tongue and kept driving. Then I began to see portions of my life flash in front of me. I got scared and started praying. God again instructed me to slow down because little of my 18-hour work days were focused on him but on worldly achievement. I decided to stop at our local hospital instead of going home. Once I exited my van the rush of cold air eliminated my discomfort. The machismo in me told me that I was OK; I was in great physical shape and didn't need to go into the emergency room. Then my reasoning kicked in and told me to enter the ER. After the normal triage, EKG, and routine tests I was ready to leave, since things appeared normal. However, I was advised to spend the night and submit to additional tests the next day. I had too much to do to stay in the hospital. Then God ordered me to stay, so I did. While in the quietness of my hospital room I realized that pride and disobedience to God's word can rob us of our health. After two days of tests, including a CT scan, stress test, and MRI, nothing was found to be abnormal. I was released and resumed my normal activities.

2. God places help along our path.

I trudged on up the long, long hill leading up to Forest Hill Avenue and the halfway point near Forest Hill Park. The halfway mark offers psychological boosts since you're half way there and the finish line is closer than the start point. And there was a big party with large crowds, cheerleaders, banners, energy drinks, water, and so on. I even had my own personal cheerer show up to spirit me on. My time looked good as I headed into the sixteenth mile across the Lee Bridge back to the north side of town. I was concerned about crosswinds on the bridge until a voice rang out, "Runners, the wind is at your back." The strong wind actually helped propel us during the uphill climb. Things were progressing well for me and I continued on. At mile 17 my legs signaled that they needed a break and commanded that I begin my walk /run routine. Not me, because I wasn't suppose to walk until mile twenty as planned. Mile eighteen was painful and slow. It seemed like an endless mile. I refused to walk even though it would have been faster since I could have at least taken full strides as opposed to my tiny running steps. Mile nineteen seemed to stretch forever and I finally reached mile twenty. I was supposed to start walking, but I couldn't. My leg muscles had seized up as a result of my stubbornness. I was finished. I stopped to stretch. But stretching did no good. I took a few more steps and stretched some more. I was reduced to painful little steps. I felt like a knocked-down boxer barely able to pick himself up off the canvas. It was time to quit. But my fellow runners said, "Keep moving." I slowly moved and decided to quit and seek medical help. But my fellow runners said, "You're almost there, keep moving." I was exhausted and noticed my body exhibiting some of the signs of heat exhaustion, but because I wasn't sweating I knew it was something else. As I went through the stone entryway into one of the final neighborhoods there was a sign reading, "You Have Not Hit the Wall." I felt like I had not only hit the wall, but the wall had fallen on me.

I had enough. I was embarrassed by my retarded movements, and trekked on with my head slung low. I just wanted to stretch out on one of the plush lawns and elevate my feet. I quit. Then a guy said, "Smile, there are cameras up ahead." A lady holding a champagne glass and partying with her neighbors gave me a big hug and asked if I wanted to stop there. I said, "No, thank you, Ma'am. I think I can make it."

I was paying the price for pride. I knew better than to let my psyche override my body's needs. There was no dishonor in walking. It is okay to slow down sometimes when necessary. It was a marathon and the point is to finish, and despite good preparation circumstances were not as anticipated. So make adjustments based on present circumstances. It was hot, it was humid, and it was windy. I knew what was happening as a result of disobedience and ignoring my body's survival signals. I wanted to throw up, but couldn't. I think I over hydrated with a sports drink. I felt bad all over. I was also feeling uneasiness in my upper left chest. Heart attack, maybe? No. I had felt the same discomfort several times during training and deep breathing had taken care of it.

I reflected back to July 11, 2003, when I woke up and was unable to get the left side of my body to function properly. Because the weakness and my slurred speech were signs of a stroke, I popped an aspirin into my mouth and headed to the emergency room. I was feeling better when I got there but went in anyway. The emergency room physician reviewed my medical history and ordered some tests. The next day I saw a neurologist. After reviewing my medical and family history, the doctor told me I needed a regimen of stroke prevention. I paid attention and followed his advice.

3. God restores our strength.

My steps got longer as the pain began to subside, but I was finished running. Still, I was going to finish the marathon even if I had to crawl to the finish line. Eventually I was on the final three-mile stretch as I walked through the campus of Virginia Union University, a historically black college and university, which grew out of the ashes of the Civil War. Among its graduates are L. Douglas Wilder, America's first elected African American governor; and Samuel L. Gravely, Jr., the Navy's first black admiral. I thought how fitting the backdrop of traversing the place where black folks overcame obstacles and life's marathons to get to the finish line. It took a lot of preparation, patience, perseverance, and sacrifice. It wasn't easy but they completed their desired journeys. They made it to the finish line that they, and not someone else, had set. They paid the price and achieved the victory.

I had to finish my marathon and was almost there. I then got a big boost. My personal cheerer appeared. She had strategically placed herself to give me that needed bit of encouragement. She walked with me awhile and told me she knew that I would finish even though she had advised me not to participate in the marathon. After making the last turn I could see the finish line and thanked my friend as I mustered up enough strength to run the final distance. I crossed the finish line with a disastrous time.

4. Trust God in all things.

I finished the 31ˢᵗ Richmond Marathon having gained a better appreciation of my life's journey. Throughout my life I was never alone. God was with me. I was surrounded by people who were with me. Strangers and well wishers were with me. That's how life is. When you are seemingly at your lowest point someone is there to lift you up. When you lack the strength and the will to go on, somehow you find just enough strength to keep moving until your will is restored. Disappointments fuel the abandonment of goals once we doubt our abilities. But there is always someone around to encourage us, to keep us focused on the goal, and to lift our spirits. We get that boost from unanticipated sources and keep moving.

In summary, throughout our lives we receive strength and encouragement from sources known and unknown. We know the story of the Man of La Manchu and hear the music of "The Impossible Dream," but do we dare to dream? We hear the lyrics but may not believe them until we step out on faith. When we elect to participate in the opportunities around us we realize that we can achieve our dreams. But one must be prepared. First there must be a strong foundation. Excavation for the footing of a building is an unglamorous but critical process. A building will not survive on a weak foundation. Therefore, if the foundation is strong, something enduring can be built on it. The best foundation is education. That diploma, degree, or certificate validates that there is a base strong enough to build on. It is evidence that the foundation can support that which is to come: education, experience, and advancement. Then opportunity begins to influence the shape of the structure on top of the strong foundation. Each structure is unique and a recognizable symbol in its own right. I encourage everyone to build a strong foundation to support life's enduring challenges and opportunities.

CHAPTER FOURTEEN

DO DADS

We have plenty of examples of successful individuals overcoming the odds. We know the stories of Ray Charles, Muhammad Ali, Attorney Willie Gary, Reginald Lewis (Harvard Law, Beatrice Foods), General Colin Powell, neurosurgeon Dr. Ben Carson, Michael Jordon, President William Clinton, and President Barack Obama. But more important, we have family, friends, and neighbors we know personally to emulate as role models. There are infinite examples. My familiar examples include a woman who had two children born out of wedlock in rapid succession before she reached voting age. She self-corrected, and eventually earned her bachelor's, master's, and doctorate degrees and placed herself in a position to help young college students maneuver their way through life. Another is a woman whose mother had three children born out of wedlock before marrying and adding another half dozen children to the family. She was the oldest child and tired of the family's unplanned moves, homelessness, and evictions. She escaped by joining the United States Air Force. After her discharge she used her educational benefits and other opportunities to earn her bachelor's degree in twenty-four continuous months and her jurist doctorate three years later. A Navy recruiter noticed the leadership potential in a high school senior right before she graduated and invited her to enlist in the Navy for its Broadened Opportunity for Officer Selection and Training Program (BOOST). She accepted the challenge and attended the United States Naval Academy Preparatory School (Prep School) following her boot camp. After Prep School she accepted a full four-year Navy ROTC scholarship, graduated from Hampton University, and was commissioned as an ensign. Following her active duty stint she earned an MBA using her educational benefits and entered the business world. There are too many examples to list. The common theme is that individuals, regardless of life's circumstances, were willing to work towards their goals one day at a time.

On January 20, 2009, Barack Obama became the 44th President of the United States of America. "Yes we can!" was the theme of his stellar presidential campaign as he energized the nation. "Yes you can!" "Yes I can!" "Yes we can!" We can do anything we chose to do individually and collectively. Now for the first time in America's history we have a President of the United States whose childhood profile resembles that of the majority of the black male prison population: absentee father and single mother low-income household. Therefore, there are no more excuses. No more excuses, as Bill Cosby has preached for years. There are no excuses for the baby makers who don't know what being a father is. The boys who engage in careless sex and make babies without any thought of taking responsibility for their actions must be held accountable. This doesn't excuse the woman who elects to get pregnant for whatever reason, since these days a woman usually only gets pregnant intentionally, perhaps in an attempt to entrap a man into a relationship.

I sense that the most cherished thing in a young child's life is the recognition of a father, or a dad, biological or appointed. Actually its daddy recognition that they crave, because a true father doesn't need any prompting to fulfill his responsibilities. Mothers, please take note. A child craves to have a daddy to identify with. The quality of the dad is immaterial. It is knowing that someone is willing to acknowledge them that is important. They will not judge their mother's decision in choosing a bed mate. The sperm donor may even be a deadbeat dad. A child seeks validation of his or her worth by a man who can be identified as Dad.

Just visit any jail or prison in America and take note of the children's excitement over seeing that physical representation of their dads. The kids are oblivious to the confinement that separates them from their fathers and clamor to be recognized by the men in prison garb during the time allowed. They will travel great distances and endure the heat and cold for their special moment. They want a photograph with Dad as proof of his existence.

Also take note of our naval bases and military installations, as the children cling to their fathers as they go to and from deployments around the globe. Then notice the warrior fathers in the news who have compassion for children everywhere and will risk everything and give anything to help a child in foreign lands.

There is one script for fatherhood. It has been written by God.